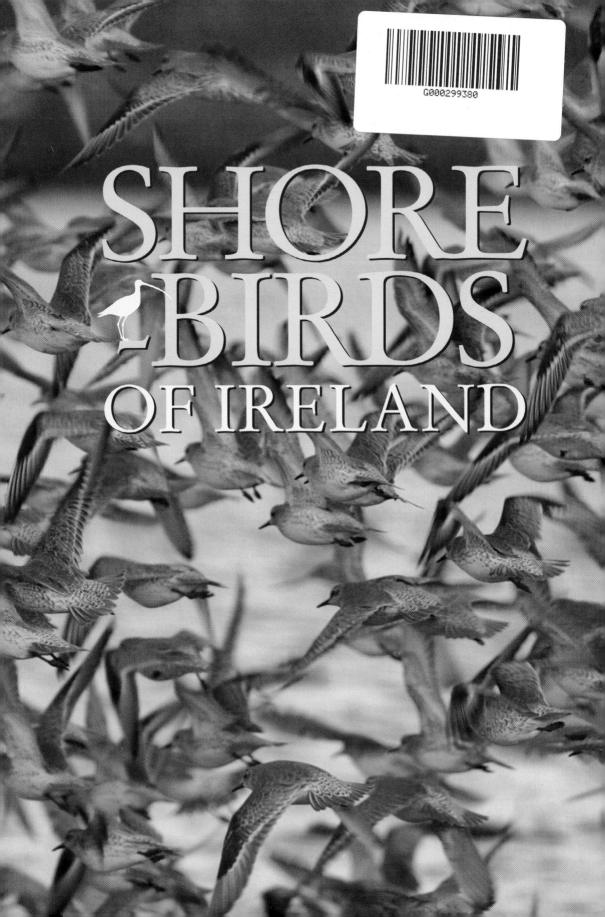

SHORE BIRDS
OF IRELAND

G000299380

Dedicated to
Clive Hutchinson (1949–1998)
A friend and inspiration

SHORE BIRDS
OF IRELAND

Text by
Jim Wilson

Images by
Mark Carmody

The Collins Press

FIRST PUBLISHED IN 2009 BY
The Collins Press
West Link Park
Doughcloyne
Wilton
Cork

© Jim Wilson and Mark Carmody 2009

Jim Wilson and Mark Carmody have asserted their moral right
to be identified as the authors of this work.

All rights reserved.
The material in this publication is protected by copyright law.
Except as may be permitted by law, no part of the material may be reproduced
(including by storage in a retrieval system) or transmitted in any form or by any means,
adapted, rented or lent without the written permission of the copyright owners.
Applications for permissions should be addressed to the publisher.

British Library Cataloguing in Publication Data
Wilson, Jim.
  The shorebirds of Ireland.
  1. Shore birds--Ireland. 2. Shore birds--Ireland--
  Identification.
  I. Title II. Carmody, Mark.
  598.3'3'09415-dc22

ISBN-13: 9781848890176

This publication has received support from the Heritage Council
under the 2009 Publications grant scheme

Design and typesetting by edit+
Typeset in Sabon and Myriad Pro
Printed in Spain by GraphyCems

FSC
Mixed Sources
Product group from well-managed
forests and other controlled sources
Cert no.TT-COC-002607
www.fsc.org
© 1996 Forest Stewardship Council

Contents

Acknowledgements

Jim would like to thank the following people for their invaluable support, help and advice in the writing of this book:

Ann, Peter and Barry for their patience and support. Mom, Dad, Margaret, Carmel, John and Mary. Pat Smiddy, Pete Potts, Ruth Croger, Elizabeth and David Price, Anne de Potier and all the Farlington Ringing Group, Tómas Gunnarsson, Daniel Hayhow, Jenny Gill, José Alves, Guillaume Gélinaud, Astrid Kant, Helen Boland and BirdWatch Ireland, Mark Grantham and the BTO, Iain Hill, Simon Delany and Wetlands International, Graham McElwaine, Kendrew Colhoun and the Irish Brent Goose Research Group, Joyce and Martin Enright, Tom Sharpe, Sarah Clarke, Sigga Beta, Willie McSweeney and pupils and staff at Scoil Iosaef Naofa Cobh, Chris Wilson, John F. Murphy and Stan Nugent of Waxwing Productions, Guðný Róbertsdóttir and Lukka Heimisdóttir and Láki Sigurbjörnsson.

Mark would like to thank the following people for their invaluable support, help, information and advice without which he would not have been able to spend countless hours in the field to capture the moments frozen in the photographs of this book:

Mary, John, Gillian, Paul, Sandro, Elia, Madeleine, Ciarán Cronin, Colin Barton, Kieran Grace, Paul Kelly, Dave Dillon, John F. Murphy, Owen Foley, and Breffni Martin, and Alan Lauder and Kathryn Finney at BirdWatch Ireland. Mark would also like to thank Jim Wilson for the inspiration to pick up a pair of binoculars when he was a young lad and introducing him to the magnificent and rewarding world of Ireland's birds.

We would both like to thank all at The Collins Press and all those who have spent long hours studying and counting shorebirds, without whom this book would not be possible.

Facing page:
A mixed flock of dunlin, sanderling and purple sandpipers flying to a high-tide roost.

Introduction

Above:
A blur of knot, one of the longest-distance migrant shorebirds.

Preceding page:
Shorebirds feeding on a rising shore. Each year Ireland's shores play host to over 1 million shorebirds.

Twice a day the tide comes in and goes out again. It symbolises the living sea, breathing in and out. As it does so it covers and uncovers a thin strip of ground around its edge. This place, which cannot be claimed to be land or sea, has become home to thousands of animal and plant species. In choosing this place to be their home they have become slaves to the ebbing and flowing tide, gathering food while they can before the tide either exposes their food to the air or puts it out of reach beneath water. One group of animals that has tied itself to the rhythms of the tide is the shorebirds. Like our ancestors, they discovered the rich food supply that the sea edge has to offer. They have evolved over millennia to take advantage of the huge variety of creatures that have also made this restless environment their home. The earliest fossil webbed footprints of a shorebird date to the Early Cretaceous period (between 146 and 100 million years ago) and these, along with non-webbed footprints from that time, suggest there was a good variety of shorebird species even then. Most shorebirds have relatively long legs to allow them to wade along the water's edge in search of those animals preparing to hide beneath the sand and mud on the falling tide or coming to the surface to feed when the sea covers them on an incoming tide.

While the definition of what is a shorebird is open to interpretation,

for the purpose of this book we consider a shorebird as a bird that is mainly found on intertidal areas around our coast. Shorebirds generally comprise waders – birds with long legs and beaks of various sizes and shapes designed to catch their prey in intertidal areas; some ducks, geese and swans, gulls and terns that spend most of their time on or near the seashore. We also include a few species that do not fit into a neat category but depend on the shore to a greater or lesser extent for their survival.

Each winter, over 20 million shorebirds fly south along the east Atlantic coast from their summer homes, many from high latitudes where they have reared a family in twenty-four hours of daylight. They are heading for places with a kinder climate and a plentiful food supply to see them through to their next breeding season. Many of those born during the summer will make the journey for the first time without the help of their parents. Over the generations they have been handed down a biological map and navigation kit that allows them to make the hazardous trip unaided. As well as those that stay here for the winter, many more use Ireland's seashore to take a brief rest and refuel before heading farther south for the winter, sometimes as far as the shores of South Africa. It is not just the swallow or the cuckoo that have discovered the advantages of this long and hazardous annual journey.

On the pages of this book, with words and images, we hope to introduce you to the beauty and wonder of Ireland's shorebirds.

Above from left:
Ireland's mudflats are vital for the survival of many of our shorebirds and a valuable part of the marine ecosystem.

Lugworm casts dot a flat sandy beach in Sligo.

Bull Island, a major site for shorebirds in Ireland, right in the heart of Dublin.

Where rock meets the ocean, an amazing array of shore habitats is created.

Geology of our Shore

The characteristic deep brown colour of peat can be clearly seen well below the high-tide line on this beach aptly named Ballinamona (the town of the bog).

The Irish coastline is over 7,000 kilometres long, longer than that of Spain or France. It has one of the highest ratios of coastline-to-land surface area of any country in the world. Huge forces have shaped today's coast, producing a rich tapestry of shore types ranging from exposed, sandy beaches and rugged, rocky shores in the west to mud-filled, sheltered estuaries and salt marshes in the east, and all combinations in between. Repeated glaciation, erosion by sea and rain, movement of submarine sediments by ocean currents, deposition of inland sediments by run-off from the land through rivers and streams, all contribute to our changing coastline.

At the end of the last ice age, some 10,000 years ago, as the weight of the enormous ice sheet was removed from the land, parts of the Irish land mass sprang back up, raising former shorelines along the northeast coast. Elsewhere, the land sank and this, coupled with the rise in sea level as the ice melted, has submerged parts of the coast. Evidence of this can be seen today in the deep, flooded valleys of the southwest and some intertidal areas in the south where peat layers and tree stumps are visible well below the current high-tide line.

All these forces, along with the composition of the shoreline rocks and sediments which has a bearing on the plants and animals that colonise them, have resulted in a wide variety of intertidal habitats which, in turn, has provided the basis for one of the richest collections of marine plants and animals. This has not gone unnoticed by passing shorebirds and they very quickly spread out to almost every part of Ireland's shoreline to take advantage of this abundant food supply.

Humans on the Shore

The archaeological record shows that the seashore has been important to us over the millennia and has been exploited in many ways. There is ample evidence to show that the seashore was a very important place in the lives of early settlers in Ireland. The first settlers on the shores of Ireland were Mesolithic hunter-gatherers who came here by sea about 10,000 years ago. The archaeological record shows that initially they settled on lake shorelines and rivers as well as near the seashore in sheltered inlets and estuaries, and caught fish and birds and gathered shellfish from the intertidal area.

Much of the evidence for this comes from the numerous rubbish heaps they left around the coastline of Ireland. These rubbish heaps are usually referred to as middens. The word 'midden' means a dunghill and 'kitchen midden' specifically means a prehistoric refuse-heap, mainly of shells and bones. These coastal middens often contain large amounts of seashells, which indicate the importance of the seashore to our ancestors' survival in their new home.

Significant archaeological evidence of our early close links with the seashore has been found in places such as Strangford Lough (Down), Dundalk Bay (Louth), the Shannon and Fergus estuaries and Castlemaine Harbour (Kerry). Bones of birds found on or near the shore, such as mallard, teal and wigeon, have been found at Ireland's oldest Mesolithic site at Mount Sandel in Derry.

These hunter-gatherers collected shellfish such as oysters, mussels, limpets, cockles, whelk, periwinkle, and even cowrie shells as well as the eggs of birds nesting along the shore. They trapped fish such as salmon and eels in estuaries and caught fish such as ballan wrasse on rocky shores. Archaeologists believe waterways, including the coast, were central to the way of life of the Mesolithic Irish settlers. Just like the shorebirds, they used the changing face of the seashore during the year to their advantage.

Finds from the Late Mesolithic Period (6000–4000 BC) include fish spears, nets, baskets and V-shaped fish traps, made of material like hazel and rushes, to catch flounder, plaice, mullet and other fish in shallow water and estuarine areas. Some of the best examples of these were found in Dublin on the Liffey estuary. Shell middens there revealed a variety of species, indicating extensive use of the intertidal area either for collecting food or bait. Another midden at Sutton in Dublin (4340–3810 BC) contained shells of over twenty shellfish species, again emphasising the use of the intertidal area for food and

An exposed 1-metre high section of the shell midden at Culleenamore, County Sligo, showing just a fraction of the millions of shells left there by early Irish settlers.

also showing how knowledgeable they were about what could be eaten from this area. Many seaweed species are very nutritious and would have also been gathered. Even for those who did not live permanently near the shore, there is evidence to show that, for generations, groups would return at certain times of the year on an annual basis, setting up temporary dwellings in order to exploit the seasonal rich food supply on the shore.

Just outside Sligo town on the shore of Ballysadare Bay is Culleenamore. There are aproximately twenty middens along an 8-kilometre stretch from Culleenamore to Ballysadare village in the bay. The midden at Culleenamore, which was actively used between about 2760 BC and 200 BC is a remarkable example of the scale of use of the seashore by our ancestors. The midden was huge, about half the size of a football pitch, and there is archaeological evidence to suggest that this was only half its original size. The shell layers in places are 3 metres deep. The midden consists mainly of oyster shells, but also includes mussels, cockles and periwinkles with occasional examples of whelk, limpet, scallop and clams too. Charcoal and hearths (fireplaces), burnt stones and unburnt animal bones and even the grave of a small child were found in the midden. Some hearths were very large and it is thought that the people spent some weeks or months on the midden in wintertime. Collections of 100 to 125 mussel and periwinkle shells were found beside the hearths and may have represented the remains of a family meal. The average shell size decreased over the years, suggesting that there may have been overexploitation of this intertidal food supply in prehistoric times.

Shorebirds must have helped Ireland's early settlers mark the

passing of the seasons as they began to arrive here in the autumn from their northern breeding grounds and return in the spring, thus signalling the approach and end of winter and the coming and going of seasonal food supplies.

As time passed, our ancestors turned from the hunter-gatherer lifestyle to one of a settled farming-based society and the links with the seashore and the sea began to fade for many Irish communities.

In the Middle Ages we exploited the ready supply of seaweed on the seashore and it was both eaten and used for fertiliser. In the seventeeth and eighteenth centuries, the harvesting of kelp was significant, and the remains of kelp walls, used to dry out kelp, and kelp kilns to reduce it to ash, are to be seen, especially on the west coast. Kelp ash, in particular, was a major money spinner: it is rich in iodine and is alkaline. Burning kelp releases the potash and soda it contains and this was used for pottery glazing and in the manufacture of glass and soap. In the early nineteenth century, a total of 60,000 tonnes of kelp was collected for iodine extraction.

By the middle of the nineteenth century, mineral substitutes were discovered and this industry faded out. Coastal communities persisted in exploiting the seashore with the collection of seaweed for fertiliser, continuing to the present day. Today, commercial harvesting of seaweed endures, especially to supply ingredients for the food and cosmetic industry. A derivative of kelp – alginate – is still used as a thickening agent in ice cream and jelly, as well as beauty products, particularly shower gels, seaweed baths and even toothpaste.

Today some people, such as these periwinkle pickers, continue to gather food from the shore.

Salt marshes are found in sheltered areas all around our coast. They are flat areas of salt-tolerant vegetation, which are covered to a greater or lesser degree at high tide and provide roosting and feeding areas for shorebirds. In the past some were used for grazing livestock and even peat extraction. As these areas are semi-land they have always been a target for 'land reclamation', (a misnomer, since many of these areas were never dry land in the first place). In the eighteenth and nineteenth centuries, many areas of salt marsh were 'reclaimed' and indeed many of our larger ports – such as Drogheda, Dublin,

Waterford, Cork and Limerick – have developed and expanded following reclamation of salt marsh and estuarine areas.

We still hunt our shorebirds, though not as extensively as in the past. Shorebirds such as the wigeon, teal and even curlew are on the hunting list in Ireland.

Today we mainly use the seashore for recreation and it has become a very important part of our tourist economy with walking, angling and birdwatching contributing to the income of many communities around our coast.

Seaweed is still harvested today for many purposes.

The Life of a Shorebird

Feeding

Just like any creature living on the planet, the behaviour of shorebirds is dictated by where they live. The tide rises and falls twice each day, allowing those animals and plants that live between the high and low tides to thrive. Shorebirds have evolved to take advantage of this rich food resource and in doing so have become locked into the rhythm of the tides, feedings when the tide recedes, and resting and grooming when the shore is under sea.

Where freshwater flows into the sea, the silts, clay and organic matter deposited in the form of mudflats provide the building blocks for a staggering array of small creatures. It has been shown that the diversity and volume of life in a square metre of mud can be as rich as that in a tropical rainforest. It is no surprise, then, that larger animals such as fish and birds have learnt to exploit this plentiful food source. To catch this food you need the right tools and shorebirds have developed tools that are perfectly suited for catching their chosen prey. One of the most important tools comes inbuilt in the form of a beak.

The beak can tell us much about a shorebird. The shape alone can give you a good indication of where and how it feeds. It ranges in shape and size from broad and flat, such as the teal's, to very long and curved ones, such as the curlew's, the shorebird with the longest beak of all Irish shorebirds.

Shorebirds have evolved two main types of feeding techniques: sight and touch. Some feed only by sight and others only by touch, while many can change between the two techniques depending on the feeding conditions.

Some wader beaks are straight and others are curved. Straight beaks are good for going deep and fast into mud or sand, while a curved beak is better for getting into out-of-the-way-places, even around corners, and for pulling long worms out of U-shaped burrows deep in mud or sand. Waders with curved beaks have shorter tongues and so have to lift and grab the prey repeatedly until it is caught by the tongue and swallowed. That is why you will often see long-billed shorebirds like the curlew and the godwit rocking their heads forward and backward with the beak opening and closing fast to move the

Facing page:
A black-tailed godwit probing for food in shallow water.

15

Above:
The beak of this black-headed gull is designed for all-purpose use to suit its broad diet.

Below:
Two black-tailed godwits fighting. The flexible beak is clearly visible on the bird to the left.

prey back towards the tongue.

Waders such as the knot or black-tailed godwit have very sensitive tips to their beaks, a bit like having an ultra-sensitive finger at the end of the hard, nail-like beak. They use this sensitive beak tip to 'see' under the mud or sand. They can detect tiny movements, such as changes in water pressure and also possibly vibrations, and know from which direction they are coming. As a result, they probe the mud or sand in the direction of the increased water pressure or vibration until they find their prey. This is why you might see a wader probing rapidly in the mud like a sewing machine needle. It is feeling its way though the mud or sand 'looking' for food.

By simply sticking its beak into the mud a knot can detect prey hiding up to 5 centimetres away. Research has shown that it is not the movement or other signs from a living creature that it senses but the disruption of water pressure on its beak by the solid object. Unfortunately, knots cannot tell a stone from a small shellfish so they learn to avoid feeding in mud or sand with lots of small stones.

In many waders, like the black-tailed

godwit, the upper part of the beak is flexible near the tip. It is thought that this is essential for catching prey deep underground. A rigid beak would be very difficult to open while pushed deep into mud of sand but the flexible tip allows the target food item to be grabbed more easily and with less energy underground. This flexible tip has also been shown to be used by smaller waders to grab small prey in water more efficiently.

Turnstones have short, wedge-shaped beaks ideal for turning over stones and seaweed in search of food while using the least amount of energy. The dunlin feeds by probing the mud or sand as many as ninety times a minute in search of the telltale signs of its prey. Waders with longer beaks tend to eat larger and less prey, buried deeper in mud and sand, than waders with smaller beaks.

Recently it has been discovered that some of the smaller waders use water surface tension to 'suck' small prey items into their mouth. By opening and closing the small tweezers-like beak, drops of water move upward towards the mouth by capillary action where the tongue can catch the food. More studies are

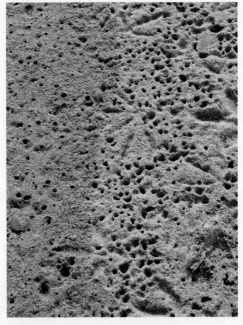

Above:
A sandy beach peppered with probe holes left by dunlin.

Below:
A purple sandpiper passes in the foreground as mud flies when a turnstone stabs at firm sand in search of food.

Clockwise from top:

Geese, swans and ducks, which do not normally dive, like this pair of pintails, will upend to get at food in deeper water.

The conical beak of a goose is designed mainly for eating plant material.

A modified photo of an oystercatcher showing how long its beak would be in just one year if it were allowed to grow required to see if this feeding mechanism is more widely used amongst shorebirds.

The beak on a shorebird is a complex combination of tiny sensory organs for hunting prey moving beneath the surface of mud, sand or water and a tough fingernail-like material that resists damage while probing and is even strong enough to withstand pounding a hard shell to get at the meat inside.

Just like our own fingernails, shorebirds' beaks are always growing, and at a faster pace than our fingernails. The beak of an oystercatcher grows nearly three times faster than our fingernails, and if it was not for the constant wear of probing in mud and sand or smashing open shellfish, in one year it would be over twice its normal length.

Ducks have developed a beak which, unlike the waders, is broad and flat. It is used to sift large quantities of small creatures such as small shellfish and crustaceans from the surface of the mud. It is also a useful shape for eating large quantities of seaweed and even grass. The shelduck, Ireland's largest duck, uses its broad, flattened beak to sieve the material on the surface of mud by moving its head from side to side in broad arcs and, with the help of special grooves inside the beak, it can separate out its food with its tongue.

Geese have beaks that are generally not as broad and flat as ducks'. The diet of the brent goose, the only member of the goose family in Ireland that can be considered a true shorebird, largely comprises various seaweeds, although in places like Dublin Bay, it has taken to grazing the grass in parks and on playing pitches.

Gulls are like the crows of the seashore, scavengers with a broad taste and their beaks are a general-purpose design, with those of the larger gulls capable of tearing flesh.

In relatively recent years, more and more brent geese are feeding on grass in playing fields and parks.

Eyes and Ears

All shorebirds have good eyesight. This is especially important when you choose to feed out in the open with nowhere to hide. Shorebirds are constantly on the lookout for danger, such as a hunting peregrine falcon or sparrowhawk. If you are dinner for one of the fastest birds on earth, seeing it before it gets too close for you to escape is the difference between life and death.

Some shorebirds mainly feed on prey that lies on the surface of mud or sand and those have relatively large eyes. One group of shorebirds, waders called plovers, have larger eyes than other waders and even much bigger birds like gulls or geese. The ringed plover is a perfect example of this, relying mainly on sight to find its fast-moving prey.

Unlike the sewing-machine action of the 'hunt by touch' experts, it is usually seen standing very still, watching for movements on the surface and then darting forward to capture its prey before it can bury

All gulls usually hunt by sight and have relatively large eyes.

itself deep into the mud or sand out of reach of the ringed plover's relatively short beak. These large eyes also allow it to see prey even in poor light conditions and to hunt more effectively at night. Other shorebirds use touch as the main way of detecting their prey. These birds tend to have relatively smaller eyes and instead rely more on the sensitive tip of their beaks to find their prey hiding beneath the mud or sand. Ducks and geese usually feed by sight but use touch to separate food from inedible material. Many of them eat mostly plant material and graze like cattle.

Ducks increase the amount of animal prey they eat as the breeding season approaches; this may be to build up strength for the rigours of migration and breeding.

All birds have ears, though they are not usually visible since they are covered by feathers. Waders have very good hearing, which enables them to detect the sound of worms and shellfish moving in the mud or sand. This might sound impossible to us but when you can get your ear within a few millimetres of the ground, a fine-tuned ear can come in very handy.

Above:
Shorebirds that hunt by sight, like this ringed plover, have larger eyes than those that usually hunt by touch.

Below:
A purple sandpiper scans the sky for a peregrine falcon.

Above from left:

Note the webbed feet of a mute swan as it comes into land. Shorebirds with webbed feet often use them as air brakes when landing.

The characteristic long legs and toes of a wading bird.

Feet

When you come equipped to hunt for your food on the seashore you may have a problem getting at your prey, especially if it lives in very soft mud. Have you ever seen someone trying to walk across soft mud? They make very hard work of it and often sink so far into the mud that they get stuck. This is because we are not designed for the job. Our weight relative to the surface area of the soles of our feet means we cannot be supported on this soft surface and are bound to sink.

Shorebirds have overcome this problem of hunting on these food-rich places. For waders, who do not have webbed feet, the bigger the bird the proportionally bigger their feet are in order to spread their body weight and prevent them from sinking. Some waders prefer sandy ground and avoid soft mud. One such species is the sanderling, which prefers sandy shores and unlike most shorebirds, has no hind toes on its feet. One suggestion is that this is probably because it does not need them since it will not sink on firm sand.

The general rule for shorebirds is the softer the ground where they hunt the bigger the feet, to spread their weight and stop them from sinking. Ducks, geese and gulls have shorter toes relative to body weight but because they have webbed feet their weight is also spread, just like someone using snowshoes on soft snow, and they do not sink or get stuck in the mud while hunting.

Dinner time

Oystercatchers spend less time hunting for food than smaller shorebirds.

Sand is not as rich in food for shorebirds as mud but some species have specialised in hunting there, such as the sanderling, bar-tailed godwit and ringed plover. You will find shorebirds exploiting available food sources on open, rocky shores, away from the shelter of bays and inlets. The most specialised of these is the purple sandpiper.

While the volume of food on a rocky shore is much less than on sand or mud there is also less competition for it as most shorebirds that specialise in feeding on mud or sand are unable to hunt the creatures that live on rocky shores.

Larger species of wader may spend as little as six hours out of twenty-four hunting, while smaller species may spend up to twelve hours out of twenty-four. This is why you might see smaller species like dunlin continue to feed until the last of the exposed shore is covered, while larger waders like curlews or oystercatchers are standing around before the tide comes in. They generally eat larger prey which is usually found lower down the shore – last to be uncovered and first to be covered.

As the days grow short and daylight decreases, unlike almost all land birds, which stop feeding after dark, many shorebirds continue to feed at night. At this time of year, for some species the energy they gain by feeding when the tide is out is only just enough to allow them to survive, so they cannot stop feeding during the hours of darkness

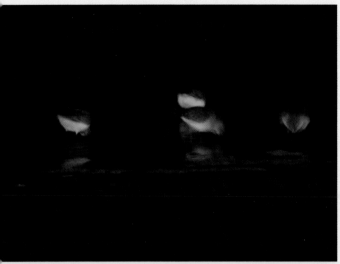

and therefore their feeding times are dictated solely by the rhythm of the tides. Some shorebirds such as oystercatcher and curlew only forage at night if they do not get enough food during the day. In winter the oystercatcher has to feed at night because it will rarely catch enough food during the one low tide in the short day. On average, they have only half the time to feed (four to five hours) in winter than in summer, so almost all have to feed at night to keep up energy levels.

Visual hunters are less likely to hunt at night than those that use touch, although some, such as the redshank, have been shown to switch from visual hunting to hunting by touch during the hours of darkness. Plovers, which are normally visual hunters, will feed on moonlit nights and where there is artificial light. There is a suggestion that some waders, such as dunlin, feed at night to avoid predators, although owls will sometimes hunt waders at night. It was found that when dunlin were disturbed while feeding at night, rather than flying away as they would during the day, they became quieter and remained motionless. It has been shown that in areas where birds are regularly shot at, they turn to feeding almost exclusively at night. The relatively recent increase in artificial light on intertidal areas has led to changes in the feeding behaviour of shorebirds that feed at night.

Research on night-feeding waders in intertidal areas illuminated by artificial light from urban areas has resulted in some interesting findings that may have a long-term impact on both the birds and their prey. Waders were attracted to areas of illuminated mud and sand and were able to eat a lot more prey than those feeding in areas unaffected by artificial illumination.

Changes in hunting behaviour were also seen. For example, redshank and dunlin, which normally feed by touch at night, were able to switch to feeding by sight. The long-term effects of ever increasing artificial illumination on shorebirds is unknown but it remains to be seen whether it will have a positive or negative effect on them and their prey. In the months leading up to spring migration, birds will feed more to put on weight by either feeding more or for longer, including at night. Instead of feeding at night some waders will switch from the shore to feeding on pasture/playing fields/parks, for crane fly larvae and earthworms, usually when the tide is high or when not enough food can be gathered on the shore.

Geese will sometimes feed at night especially when there is a full moon in the sky. Research has shown that ducks regularly feed at night. Gulls, too, will feed at night, especially where there is artificial light. Feeding at night means less risk from predators as almost all hunt only during daylight hours.

Waders hunt for food that gives the best return for effort, so they will not always go for the biggest or smallest cockle or crab because there is too much energy expended in getting at the edible bits: they are very choosy unless starving. This is exactly the same as a person eating bite-size pieces of food rather than tiny pieces or pieces that are too big to swallow. Many shorebirds eat shell and all which is then crushed in the bird's muscular gizzard. Knot have been recorded eating, on average, one small shellfish every twelve seconds.

Amongst the shorebirds, male ducks and geese tend to be a bit bigger (occasionally much bigger) than females, while female waders are generally bigger than male waders. Female oystercatchers have longer beaks than males and spend more time than males feeding on earthworms on grass at high tide because their longer beaks help them catch the worms more easily than the males. On the other hand, the males' beaks are, on average, not only shorter but stronger. Males spend more time eating shellfish with hard shells than females because shorter beaks are better for more forceful extraction of shellfish from shells.

The advantage of a long beak is that deeper and larger prey can be caught more easily, but the disadvantage is that if the prey lives on or very near the surface and/or is small, a long beak is more awkward to use and gathering food is more time consuming. In the study of

Facing page, top:
Dunlin feeding at night by the light of street lamps.

Middle:
A dunlin probes deep into the sand.

Bottom:
A turnstone about to eat a small crab.

many animal species, including birds, there is a scientific term called 'handling time', which is the time it takes a bird from finding prey to swallowing it. The ideal prey is one with a short handling time and a high energy value.

If catching and eating prey has a long handling time then the energy reward must be high because of the amount of time and energy required to eat the prey, i.e. quality not quantity. Where handling time is short, the energy value of the prey need not be as high as less time and energy is required to eat it, i.e. quantity not quality.

Brent geese eat vegetable matter and graze just like cows. Because of this they have big stomachs and long digestive tracts to allow the vegetable matter to be digested. Because vegetable matter is much lower in energy by weight than meat, they have to eat large quantities and so, unlike shorebirds that eat meat in the form of shellfish or worms, they spend a larger part of their day feeding.

If you are eating meat, worms are reasonably straightforward to digest but if your prey is shellfish then there is the problem of dealing with their protective shells. Some shorebirds, such as purple sandpipers and knot, eat whole shellfish. In these birds a very muscular organ called the gizzard, found just before the stomach, can actually crush the shells, allowing the meat inside to be easily digested. The crushed shells then pass harmlessly through the bird's digestive system. The stomach of a knot is almost twice as heavy as that of similar-sized waders that eat prey without shells. This additional weight is muscle needed to be able to crush shellfish eaten whole. This means shorebirds such as knot do not have to worry about roughage. Those that eat only soft prey get their roughage by finding and swallowing small bits of shell and large grains of sand. Some shorebirds like the oystercatcher, which eat fairly large shellfish, break them open first and then eat the meat. Shelduck feed on smaller prey items but with their sifting technique, they can hoover up more of these and faster.

Dining on raw seafood all the time means consuming rather a lot of salt. As with humans, high salt levels can be very dangerous to a shorebird. Shorebirds, like seabirds, have developed special 'salt glands' in their heads and excess salt is excreted through their nostrils. So if you look at them closely, they often look like they have a cold, with a runny nose.

When hunting on the shore there is nowhere to hide: everyone can see what you are catching and trying to eat. The longer the handling time of your prey, the greater the chance of it being robbed. If you have to spend a lot of time getting at the meat of a large shellfish like a mussel, the risk of it being stolen increases a great deal. Black-headed

Shelduck sifting for food on an incoming tide.

gulls are well known for what is called kleptoparasitism. The gull will wait around until a wader like an oystercatcher finds a large worm and will then try to steal it off the wader before it has a chance to swallow it. Herring and common gulls can sometimes get all their food on the shore by robbing oystercatchers. The rule of eating for shorebirds is to get the food into your stomach as quickly as possible. On the shore, there is usually a hierarchy amongst the birds of a species present, with those farther up the pecking order more inclined to bully others and rob their food. Amongst oystercatchers, it is usually older birds that are found on mussel beds, as younger birds are too slow to eat them and are robbed all the time. The young ones stay out on the mud feeding on buried shellfish and only move to the mussel beds once the adults leave for the breeding grounds. They then have time to practice extracting mussels from their shells without being bothered by the adults and so will be faster and better prepared to cope when the adults return to the mussel beds the following winter. Lapwings and golden plover deter black-headed gulls from stealing their food by eating smaller prey whenever the gulls are nearby because it is not worth the gulls' time to rob such small prey items. Because of the unreliability of abundance of any one species of prey from year to year, almost all waders are not too fussy about their food, but they do have preferences.

Some waders, like curlew, have been shown to defend a winter-feeding territory on the shore every year. Waders are generally site-faithful, staying on the same area of shore for the winter, but will move if preferred food becomes scarce. Extreme weather conditions (wind and cold) can prevent shorebirds from feeding and, if prolonged for even a few days, may cost them their lives, especially in the middle of winter.

Birds tend to feed where the highest density of food is found rather than being randomly spread out across terrain that all looks the same. It has been shown that waders such as knot can remember the good spots for feeding on a mudflat and do not simply drop in anywhere.

If you want to feed on prey that can hide quickly if disturbed, for example ragworm, then you do not want other birds disturbing them while you are hunting. Studies have shown that in areas where such prey was at a high density, curlews made more frequent visits of short duration rather than fewer visits of longer duration in the hope that the prey would resurface and so be caught. The theory is that too many curlews in these areas for prolonged periods would disturb their prey too much, and hence would not resurface. Sanderling, curlew and grey plover have been observed defending the same patch of mud/sand throughout the winter and even in subsequent winters. No wader species is consistently territorial but individuals of all species can be. Different wader species that eat the same prey have evolved to avoid direct competition by hunting the same prey at different stages in its development, i.e. knot, oystercatcher and curlew eat successively bigger shellfish of the same species. Occasionally, different shorebirds actually cooperate when hunting. One form of cooperative feeding is when greenshanks and little egrets hunt for shrimps in low-tide pools. Both shrimp and fish hide by burying themselves in the sand. Collectively the birds exhaust the fleeing shrimps or small fish by constantly disturbing them and the prey is then easily caught.

Shellfish and worms multiply and are at their most numerous during the summer. So while the shorebirds are on their high-latitude breeding grounds, their winter prey in intertidal areas – worms and shellfish, etc. – can restock. This keeps the whole system ticking over.

Shorebirds rely on different parts of an estuary or shoreline at different parts of the day and year. As we see them, mudflats, sandy beaches or rocky shores are not 'all the same', a point often made by those wanting to 'reclaim' wetlands saying that there are plenty more places for the wildlife. It is a bit like destroying someone's bathroom or kitchen and saying there are plenty more rooms in the house.

Top:

Seashore creatures, like these cockles and flat periwinkles, can sustain the feeding pressure of our shorebirds by building up numbers while almost all shorebirds are on their breeding grounds in summer.

Bottom:

Lug worm casts, the telltale signs of a healthy beach.

Plumage

The beautiful colours and patterns on the plumage of an American wigeon.

A shorebird's plumage serves a number of functions: flight, heat regulation, waterproofing and buoyancy, camouflage and attracting a mate. Once they are getting enough energy in the form of food, birds are able to help regulate their body temperature with their feathers. When they are cold and want to retain as much heat as possible, they can raise the feathers to trap warm air coming from the skin thus acting as insulation for the body. If they get too hot, they can either flatten the feathers or raise them enough to let the body heat out. This is important because a shorebird has the same suit of feathers whether sitting on a nest in sub-zero temperatures in the high Arctic or looking for their next meal on a tropical, sandy beach in the hot midday sun. Ducks, geese and gulls also use the air trapped between their body and their feathers to add extra buoyancy when swimming.

In general the smaller the bird the more sensitive it is to cold, so the smaller waders on average have a tougher time keeping warm in cold weather than larger ones. Purple sandpipers, which do not migrate as far south in the winter as other waders, have more efficient heat-insulating plumage than other shorebirds, which helps them to withstand the cold better.

A feeding purple sandpiper showing the typical winter plumage of a wader.

Small shorebirds tend to have dull plumage in winter to help them blend with the greys and browns of mud, sand, rock and seaweed.

Come summer they moult some of their feathers to become more colourful to attract a mate and send out a signal to neighbours that they are holding a territory.

Larger shorebirds have few, if any, predators to worry about in winter and do not need to blend with their surroundings as much as smaller ones. They are, therefore, usually more brightly coloured all year round.

Feathers are made from the same material as human hair and, just like hair, feathers suffer from wear and tear. Our hair is always in pretty good condition because it is constantly growing and so damaged tips are quickly replaced. Unlike our hair, the feathers of all shorebirds do not grow continuously but stop growing once they reach full size, for example this takes twenty to thirty days for grey plover. Because of this, they are not continuously replacing broken or damaged ones (although, if a bird loses a whole feather, a new one usually grows in its place pretty much straightaway).

Exposure to the sun and the elements causes feather colours to fade and lighter-coloured areas to become more brittle than darker areas. To ensure they have good enough feathers for flying and insulation at all times, shorebirds will replace or moult all their feathers at least once a year. Unlike the replacement of a lost feather, moult involves all or a significant number of feathers being replaced gradually in specific order, with new feathers pushing out the old

There are twenty-two turnstones in this image. With their dark winter plumage all but two are blending perfectly with the seaweed surroundings.

feathers as they start to grow. This is usually why you sometimes see birds flying about with a number of wing and tail feathers missing. Ducks and geese usually moult their flight feathers all at once and are actually flightless (or all but flightless) for up to three weeks while the new ones grow. It is thought that they can afford to do this because, unlike other shorebirds, they can stay on open water where they are safe from almost all predators and are still able to feed during this vulnerable time. For many ducks the female moults her wing feathers later than the male, waiting until the young are independent. In many duck species the male is much more brightly coloured than the female. To help avoid detection by predators during the flightless period they replace these bright-coloured feathers with much duller ones. Shelduck are unusual among our shorebirds when it comes to moulting. They undertake what is called moult migration. Almost the entire European population of shelduck flies to Heligoland, around the Elbe Delta off northern Germany, each autumn after breeding to moult, returning to their wintering and breeding grounds when the moult is complete. No one is quite sure why they do this but it is thought that Heligoland has become a traditionally safe place for them to moult. Some other shorebirds use traditional moulting places but none as dramatically as the shelduck.

Unlike ducks and geese, waders cannot rest in relative safety on water or hide in a reed bed at this time and so they replace flight feathers gradually, and can fly even during moult. Some waders can suspend or pause their moult during migration. They usually replace

Clockwise from above:

A turnstone in its dull winter plumage looks beautiful when viewed close up.

An adult black-tailed godwit in breeding plumage feeds alongside one in non-breeding plumage.

The young brent goose on the right can be easily told from the adult on the left by the pale edges to its wing feathers.

their flight feathers once they have finished their migration from the breeding grounds. Unlike ducks and geese, waders usually moult just their body feathers from their relatively drab winter plumage into more colourful breeding plumage in the spring just before flying north to the breeding grounds. The annual moult pattern for waders and gulls is usually the replacement of head and body feathers only in the spring and then all feathers in autumn.

Shorebirds must keep their feathers in good condition: it is literally a matter of life and death. It is therefore no surprise to see them preening a lot, especially when roosting at high tide. They even have a built-in supply of feather conditioner and waterproofing in the form of a fatty liquid stored in a special preen gland at the base of the tail. If you watch shorebirds preening you will see them rub their beak and head along the base of their tail. They use the beak to transfer the preen oil to the feathers. Flight feathers get special attention and are individually oiled.

A grey heron calling loudly.

Communication

Unlike land birds, shorebirds have nowhere to hide when they are feeding, roosting or rearing their young. This has shaped the way they communicate. They communicate through sound and vision. Aural communication is important all year round; visual communication is most important during courtship and breeding. As with any study of other animals, we undoubtedly miss an array of more subtle aural and visual communication methods used by shorebirds.

Unlike songbirds such as robins and finches, it is thought that shorebird calls and songs have evolved very slowly over millions of years. This is because, unlike songbirds, shorebirds – and waders in particular – do not learn their adult song: they are born with it and it does not develop any further as they mature. It has also been found that again, unlike songbirds, shorebird calls and songs show little or

33

no detectable variation across their geographical range, i.e. they do not have regional accents, which songbirds do.

Most shorebirds are very vocal and their calls travel far across open ground. This means that if danger is approaching, all members of a flock feeding on the shore can be quickly alerted to the danger. One of the main predators of shorebirds is the peregrine falcon. It specialises in descending at high speed over a shore or estuary in the hope of outflying a shorebird. The loud call of a redshank or curlew will not only alert others of its own species but also birds of other species present. These loud calls usually result in every shorebird taking to the air. If you are walking along a shore and, for no apparent reason, every bird in the area suddenly takes to the air, look to the sky and you might see a peregrine diving at great speed into the middle of a flock. Simple maths shows us that the chance of any individual bird being caught by a bird of prey goes down as the number of birds taking flight goes up, so it is in every shorebird's interest to alert as many other birds as possible to the danger. The downside of using this strategy to survive predator attack is that shorebirds, and waders in particular, are very nervous and false alarms regularly occur when a bird might think it sees danger coming, sounds the alarm, and every bird in the area unnecessarily takes to the air.

Studies have shown that peregrine falcons usually catch young or weak individuals who are either inexperienced or not quick enough off the mark to avoid capture. Many shorebirds travel in flocks and they communicate using flight calls. Flight calls help the flock to stay together, especially when travelling at night or in poor visibility.

Here in Ireland we rarely get a chance to hear shorebirds singing on their breeding grounds. They usually sing in the air or from a vantage point so others of the same species can hear them. Most

Below from left:
A redshank calls loudly from a fence post in the evening sun.

Oystercatchers piping with necks stretched and beaks pointing to the ground.

waders have very loud and complex songs, which can sound very different from the shorter, simpler calls made here during the winter.

Unlike songbirds, shorebirds usually rely more heavily on visual displays when attracting a mate, setting up a territory or deterring predators. Many waders use aerial displays during the breeding season to signal their presence to potential partners and to ward off other males and predators. When you do not have a tall tree on your territory, the only way to signal your presence to others is by flying up into the air. Many waders perform aerial displays ranging from the complex display flight of the male lapwing which includes a 'butterfly flight' on slow, deep, wingbeats, followed by a zigzag flight which is accompanied by a humming sound produced by its wing feathers, and finally followed by climbs and dives and some singing. Visual displays on the ground can be equally perplexing: for example, five different aggressive displays have been identified in the black-tailed godwit, involving leg stretching, wing stretching, neck stretching, feather ruffling and crouching.

The heavy weight of ducks and geese relative to their wing area, known as high wing loading, means they have to flap their wings a lot more and so are not as agile as waders. As a result they tend to do most of their visual displays on the water, although they do sometimes display on land. The water-based displays are mainly used in courtship and defence of territory during the breeding season. Aerial displays are confined to simple 'unusual' flight such as slow, deliberate wing flaps with the neck stretched. On the water, visual displays of courtship and aggression have become very complicated, involving every conceivable contortion of the displaying bird's body and even water flicking with the beak.

Below from left:
Black-headed gulls call a lot when feeding in flocks.

A whimbrel sings in the evening sun over its territory in Iceland.

A male shelduck displays on the ground by stretching its head up and back.

Facing page:
Knot find safety in numbers and sometimes gather in huge flocks on estuaries.

This page, from top:
A mixed flock of dunlin, sanderling and purple sandpipers flying to a high-tide roost.

A flock of brent geese flying in V-formation.

Shorebirds will often feed in mixed groups such as these turnstones, dunlin and purple sandpipers.

Social life – Roosting and Flock Behaviour

Most shorebirds do not feed once the tide comes in and covers up their prey. They usually use this time to rest and groom themselves. Unlike land birds, shorebirds cannot roost or hide in bushes or trees and they usually gather in large groups in the open. Ducks and geese, being good swimmers, will usually rest in a group on water away from the shore. Waders, on the other hand, usually only swim when they have to and so gather at traditional land-based, high-tide roost locations. These are mostly very small islands, exposed rocks or long spits of land with little or no vegetation stretching out into the sea.

During spring tides when the water level can be much higher than usual, especially in wet and/or windy weather, waders will roost at less favourable but more sheltered sites, sometimes away from the shore. Golden plover, on the other hand, which usually feed away from the shore, often relying on large, flat mud or sandy areas exposed at low tide for roosting. These traditional sites are chosen because they afford a good all-round view so that approaching danger can be easily seen. There is safety in numbers. Roosting in a flock also reduces heat loss by an individual. Some studies suggest that birds that roost together like this also exchange information through visual cues. For example, it is thought they may be able to tell how well another individual fed while the tide was out. If a neighbour at a roost looks 'content and happy' this might mean it is finding plenty of food and it might be worth following on the next falling tide to avail of a better meal. Conversely, birds in poor condition might be avoided.

Like most birds, shorebirds do not sleep like we do. It has been shown that they are able to rest different parts of the brain at different times during a resting period. Because they cannot hide while resting, they have to remain aware at all times to avoid predators. If you look closely at a roosting flock of shorebirds you will see that none of them rarely, if ever, has both eyes closed and usually there is one eye scanning the surroundings and the sky above for danger. Waders regularly roost on one leg, as do ducks, geese and gulls when roosting on land. Birds lose most of their heat through their legs and beaks and so try to keep them covered while resting. Sitting on the ground on cold winter days would result in more heat loss than standing, causing long legs to cramp and making a quick escape more difficult, so they usually tuck one leg in under their belly feathers and tuck their beak under their wings. A wader that is disturbed when roosting will often hop, take off and land without moving the tucked up leg thus giving

the impression of having only one leg.

A large flock of shorebirds in flight is an amazing spectacle. Shorebirds such as dunlin and knot fly close together in a group when a predator is about and there can be thousands of birds in the air flying at speed. They look like a seemingly coordinated mass that can twist and turn in a synchronised way with none of the individuals appearing to crash into each other or turning the wrong way, causing the flock to break up. Much study has been carried out on the dynamics and mechanisms that make a flock of waders behave in this way. There is broad agreement that this behaviour is used to confuse and deter an aerial predator such as a sparrowhawk.

The flock acts like a single, giant organism, twisting and turning, changing shape and colour as it moves across the shore. It attempts to confuse the predator, to make it indecisive and unsure of which individual to target during its attack and reducing dramatically the chances of any individual being singled out and caught by the predator.

It is thought that the way birds fly like this is not because there is

Clockwise from left:
A rising tide pushes waders up the shore.

Fleeing a predator, such as a merlin, as part of a flock instead of flying on your own reduces your chances of being caught.

A roosting flock of bar-tailed godwits with beaks tucked.

A flock of knot 'wheel', rolling from one side to the other in flight, making the flock change colour from dark (top) to light (bottom).

a lead bird that knows what it is doing, which all the other individuals in the flock are following; rather, it is like a person driving a car in heavy traffic, adjusting speed and direction to avoid bumping into the car ahead while trying to move as fast as possible in safety. Unlike the person in the car who has to watch only the direction and speed of the car in the lane ahead the shorebird has to watch those on either side of it, as well as above and below. Just like people in traffic, birds do occasionally bump into each other in these tight flocks.

Migration

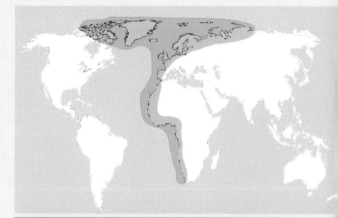

Based on fossil and geological research, migration is thought to have started to evolve between 40 and 25 million years ago. From about 15 million years ago global cooling resulted in an increase in seasonality which has remained ever since. There have been twenty-two interglacial periods in the last 20 million years. Over these very long periods of time, migration routes would have evolved very slowly in response to gradual climate change, resulting in distances between best breeding and feeding habitats increasing and decreasing over thousands of years. It is a bit like having your local supermarket moved a bit farther away every time you need to get food. If this happened over a period of thousands of years, as a species you would eventually over time, adapt to travelling the longer and longer distance. It is thought that current migration pathways started to evolve at the end of the last ice age and are less than 10,000 years old. There are still many gaps in our knowledge of the evolution of these remarkable journeys. For most shorebirds these movements appear to be programmed into their genes and they can be switched on and off as needed; but birds cannot adapt easily to short-term climatic changes.

Today migratory shorebirds migrate between breeding and non-breeding areas along generally consistent routes and, for conservation purposes, these have been broadly grouped into 'flyways'. A flyway has been defined as 'the entire range of a migratory bird species (or groups of related species or distinct populations of

From top: East Atlantic Flyway.
A paler looking bar-tailed godwit from Siberia roosts alongside black-tailed godwits from Iceland.

a single species) through which it moves on an annual basis from the breeding grounds to non-breeding areas, including intermediate resting and feeding places as well as the area within which the birds migrate'. Ornithologists recognise as many as ten major flyways around the world and migratory shorebirds seen in Ireland, which account for the vast majority of shorebirds we see, use what is called the East Atlantic Flyway, which stretches from northeast Canada across to central Siberia and south as far as South Africa.

Many attempts have been made to estimate the number of migratory birds using this flyway and a conservative estimate would suggest over 20 million shorebirds use the East Atlantic Flyway each year.

Shorebirds are attracted to Arctic and subarctic areas of the world where breeding conditions are ideal – plenty of suitable breeding places, large amounts of food for hungry chicks, more hours of daylight, fewer predators, less disease and fewer parasites. The northern summers are short, although partly compensated for by almost twenty-four hours of daylight and, incredibly, most shorebirds are able to find a nest, mate, lay eggs and rear young to fledging in the space of eight to ten weeks.

Long-toed stints like this one, which normally spend the winter in Southeast Asia and Australia, have ended up in Ireland.

For many shorebirds, males will arrive on the breeding grounds first, set up and defend a breeding territory and wait for the females to arrive. After breeding, many female waders head for the wintering grounds shortly after the eggs are laid or have hatched; the males tend to the chicks until they have fledged, and then migrate. Sometimes the female will remain with the male during this time. Finally, the fledged young are the last to leave and make the journey, unaided, to their wintering grounds, sometimes over 10,000 kilometres away.

Geese usually migrate as a family unit after the breeding season and stay together throughout the winter, only breaking up as spring approaches. Ducks are not so family orientated and by the time the young have fledged the parents have often split up.

You may well ask what triggers these birds to migrate and how do they manage to find their way between their breeding and wintering grounds along their migration routes. A lot of research has gone into answering this question and, while there is still a lot to be learned, we do have some idea of how it works. As spring approaches, length of daylight and temperature changes trigger increases in certain hormones which seem to kick-start the shorebird's migration engine. A combination of hormone levels and suitable weather conditions

Up to 80 per cent of the world's light-bellied brent geese stop off in Strangford Lough in County Down in autumn before most spread out to spend the winter on other Irish estuaries.

drive the birds to begin their migration.

Many shorebirds can migrate either by day or night and research has shown that the birds navigate using a selection of in-built instruments and visual signposts. These include interpreting the earth's magnetic field, the position of stars and geographical features. The birds are genetically programmed to fly in the right direction. Occasionally some birds get their migration wires crossed and undergo what ornithologists term 'reverse migration' where a bird, usually a young one on its first migration, migrates in the opposite direction to the one in which the species normally migrates.

Studies have revealed another interesting migration phenomenon in shorebirds, called abmigration. This occurs when a bird born in Ireland falls in with the 'wrong crowd' and gets caught up in a flock of its own species from places as far away as Siberia. The local bird either pairs up with a bird from Siberia on the wintering grounds or simply follows that flock and ends up in Siberia where it then breeds, unlike most Irish-born shorebirds that will eventually breed close to where they were born.

Travelling in flocks can help to make the journey easier. For example, a bird flying on its own will use a lot more energy than one travelling in formation in a flock. It is possible to tell if a bird is a long-distance traveller or not by the shape of its wings. In general the longer and more pointed the wing the farther the bird flies. So it is no surprise that shorebirds tend to have relatively long, pointed wings. When migrating, they will try to avoid flying into a strong wind as this uses up valuable energy. Some also use rising warm air to allow them to climb to high altitudes of over 3,000 metres where they pick up strong tail winds or are able to fly or glide 'down hill'.

Birds travelling even a short distance need plenty of fuel for the journey in the form of body fat. Some shorebirds that perform long-

Facing page:
Many shorebirds use the moon and stars to navigate during migration.

Below from left:
The red-necked stint, a rare visitor to Ireland, breeds in eastern Eurasia and spends the winter season in Southeast Asia and Australasia, as far south as Tasmania and New Zealand.

Many shorebirds migrate at night and leave in flocks at dusk.

distance migrations put on so much fat that they almost double their weight before beginning migration. Just like a pilot of an aeroplane concerned about the weight of her/his cargo, a migrating shorebird avoids carrying unnecessary weight as this requires more fuel or energy in the form of fat to be transported in flight. Research has shown that to keep their 'baggage' weight down shorebirds undergo a number of physiological changes which maximise their flying power while minimising excess weight. For example, they are able to time the increase or decrease in size of their reproductive organs so they only carry them around in fully functioning condition for the breeding season! It is thought that most only become fertile soon after they arrive on the breeding grounds.

For thousands of years millions of shorebirds have used Ireland as a winter resort with enough food and shelter here to see them through the winter when their breeding grounds are devoid of food, freezing cold and, in many places, in almost total darkness. At times Ireland also becomes a short-term refuge for tens of thousands of shorebirds moving from continental Europe during cold snaps when finding food there becomes almost impossible. Most of these birds return to their normal wintering grounds once the cold spell has past. Ireland is a vital stepping stone between breeding grounds to the north and wintering grounds farther south.

Part of a large flock of black-tailed godwits getting ready to migrate north to Iceland to breed.

Lost Souls and Pioneers – Long-distance Travellers, Unusual Visitors, American Vagrants

Each spring and autumn millions of shorebirds migrate between their wintering grounds in temperate, subtropical and tropical areas of the world and their breeding grounds in Arctic and subarctic areas. Spring migration is carried out by adults who made the same journey in previous years and young who have been lucky enough to survive their first year out of the nest on the wintering grounds.

Ireland is at the northern or western limit of the migration routes of many shorebird species and we regularly play host to a small number of birds such as avocet and black-winged stilt that have strayed just a little outside their normal range, usually during spring migration.

Autumn migration on the other hand involves far greater numbers as it is not only carried out by the breeding adults but also by all the young born that year that have survived life in the nest. Every year as all these birds pour south through the world's flyways they sometimes encounter weather systems that blow them off course.

Others, such as the inexperienced, young 'first timers' just take a wrong turn, and as a result shorebirds from many parts of the northern hemisphere end up in Ireland. For example, shorebirds flying south along the east coast of North America or heading across the Gulf of Mexico for central and South America regularly end up

Below from left:
A young American little blue heron, the first to be identified in Ireland, seen at Letterfrack, County Galway, in October 2008. It does not turn blue until it becomes an adult.

A bird with ridiculously long legs, the black-winged stilt, a rare visitor to Ireland.

here, especially in the autumn.

Shorebirds from Siberia that spend the winter in Southeast Asia and Australia occasionally end up here. As mentioned earlier this is a result of 'reverse migration' where the bird's inbuilt map and navigation system malfunctions and the bird ends up flying in the opposite direction: instead of flying southeast, they fly northwest and end up in northern Europe where they then either join birds of the East Atlantic Flyway and head south through Europe or are blown south by weather systems in the area at the time.

The numbers of these 'vagrant' birds that arrive in Ireland vary from year to year, depending on the weather and the number of birds moving south. For example, 2008 was one of the best years ever for rare North American shorebirds in Ireland. Up to 130 individuals of 18 different shorebird species were reported. This would only be a fraction of the total number to have arrived on our shores as most would go unnoticed.

There are a number of 'hot spots' in Ireland where rare shorebirds turn up. These include Ballycotton in County Cork and Tacumshin in County Wexford. Not surprisingly, because of our prevailing winds, most turn up along our south and west coast, although they can show up

From top:

An avocet with its distinctive upturned beak, hunting in shallow water. They are rare in Ireland but breed as close as England.

One of a small number of American semipalmated sandpipers that end up on Irish shores nearly every autumn.

The rare ivory gull has turned up on Irish shores on seventeen occasions and is more at home stealing scraps from polar bears in the Arctic.

The rare American wigeon sometimes comes to Ireland in the company of its Eurasian cousins.

almost anywhere in Ireland where there is a shoreline. Because of these most will spend the rest of their lives on this side of the Atlantic.

There are a few cases of American shorebirds returning to the same place in Ireland each autumn and spending the whole winter here. These birds have probably followed the migration paths of their west European cousins, flying north with them in spring and returning to their new wintering ground in Ireland each autumn. Unfortunately, it is unlikely that they breed as they would have to find a mate on this side of the Atlantic. However, some American shorebirds, like the spotted sandpiper and pectoral sandpiper, have bred or attempted to breed in Scotland. There are so many ring-billed gulls from North America in Ireland each winter that the chances of them breeding here are high, if, indeed, they have not done so already. There is a slim chance that some may get back to America if they migrate north to high enough latitudes to allow them to re-orientate and fly down the west side of the Atlantic instead of the east. They have no problem finding food here and starvation is unlikely. Shorebirds are social creatures so if their European cousins do not accept them as one of their own this might reduce their chances of survival.

A buff-breasted sandpiper looks at home on an Irish beach in the autumn but should be in North America heading for Argentina.

Facing page:
An Irish little egret chick tests its wings in Cork city on a July morning in 2009, a sight not seen in Ireland before 1997.

Left:
American ring-billed gulls are now seen here in Ireland in small numbers in winter and may even be breeding.

The breeding and wintering ranges of our shorebirds expand and contract in response to changes in climate, which affect things like suitable breeding habitat and food. Global warming has led to a number of shorebirds expanding their breeding ranges northward in the last thirty years and a few are now seen here often and are breeding here.

Two species that fit this bill are the mediterranean gull and the little egret, both of which were rare in Ireland in the 1970s. Both were recorded breeding for the first time in Ireland in 1995 and 1997 respectively and are now seen regularly. It is very possible that these are only the first of many species that will come and go in years to come.

Honorary Shorebirds

The birds that use our intertidal areas have evolved to take full advantage of the food to be found there. What most of them have in common is they do not mind getting their feet wet or muddy! Having said that, there are a few 'land birds' that spend a good deal of time hunting on the shore. The rock pipit is a relative of the wagtail and is the Irish land bird with one of the best claims to being an honorary shorebird. It lives along the shoreline and nests close by. Rock pipits are resident and rarely stray far from where they were born. Like the waders, ducks and geese, they make the most of the rich supply of food to be found on the shore.

The shore is an important place in autumn for many migrating land birds such as the swallow and the northern wheatear. In Ireland, northern wheatears nest in crevices and holes in upland rocky slopes, mainly in the west. In the autumn they migrate south for the winter.

Northern wheatears from as far away as Labrador and other parts of eastern Arctic Canada, Greenland and Iceland pass through Ireland every September and early October heading south. These birds, standing on the edge of the North Atlantic Ocean, need to take on a lot of fuel in the form of fat to make their annual journey to their wintering grounds in Africa south of the Sahara desert. To these long-distance migrants, just like their shorebird cousins, Ireland is a vital refuelling stop. The sea around our coast throws up seaweed onto the high-tide line and insects such as kelp flies feed and lay their eggs in it. The northern wheatears stop on the seashore to gorge themselves on these flies and their eggs. Without this rich shoreline food source, many wheatears would not live to reach their wintering grounds.

Often persecuted by humans, the hooded crow spends a lot of time on the seashore. Unlike the northern wheatear it does not mind getting its feet wet. It can be seen closely examining every rock crevasse and sandy area for telltale signs of a shellfish such as a cockle or mussel. Once it has found one, it has to break open the shell to get at the meat inside. A hooded crow will fly straight up, to a height of 5 to 10 metres above rocks, and drop the shellfish in the hope of cracking it open. This sometimes takes two or three tries. Once it has successfully extracted and eaten the shellfish meat, the search is on again for the next meal. Some hooded crows have taken to smashing open the shellfish on coast roads nearby. This is often the explanation for mysterious scatterings of broken shells on these roads.

Facing page, from top:
Pied wagtails, more usually seen in urban and suburban areas will sometimes feed on insects on seaweed.

A northern wheatear on its way south to Africa stops off on the shore to feed on insects in the seaweed.

How Long Do Shorebirds Live?

The seashore can be a harsh environment in which to live: exposed to the elements all the time and also exposed to predators. If you had to choose a place to live to ensure that you survived to a ripe old age, the last place you would choose would be the seashore. You might think an ideal place would be somewhere like woodland where there would be lots of food and plenty of places to rear a family, hide from predators and be protected from the cold, wind and rain. Data from ringing studies show that when the lifespan of shorebirds is compared with birds of a similar size in woodland, the shorebirds that reach adulthood on average live longer than their woodland counterparts. For example: robin – eleven years, dunlin – twenty-eight years, blackbird – twenty-one years, knot – twenty-seven years, rook – twenty-two years, and oystercatcher – forty-three years.

One theory suggests that a factor contributing to shorebirds having an increased lifespan is that there are fewer harmful bacteria and other disease-causing agents on the seashore than in other bird habitats. As with most birds, getting to adulthood is the tough part and studies have shown that for predators such as peregrines, sparrowhawks and merlins, a large proportion of the shorebirds they catch are young birds. Adults are vulnerable to predators all the time but the experience gained on the way to adulthood helps them to avoid being killed. Another factor affecting survival is the weather. Redshanks, for example, have been shown to be very susceptible to sharp drops in temperature, resulting in them being unable to catch enough food to keep them alive.

The oystercatcher holds the record for being the oldest known wader.

Longevity Records for European Shorebirds

Little Egret	22yrs 4mths *	**Black-tailed Godwit**	23yrs 6mths **
Grey Heron	35yrs 1mths *	**Bar-tailed Godwit**	>33yrs 1mths **
Brent Goose	28yrs 8mths *	**Whimbrel**	16yrs 1mths *
Shelduck	24yrs 9mths ***	**Curlew**	>31yrs 10mths ‡
Wigeon	34yrs 8mths *	**Redshank**	>26yrs 11mths ***
Teal	>21yrs 3mths *	**Greenshank**	>24yrs 5mths †
Mallard	23yrs 3mths *	**Common Sandpiper**	>14yrs 6mths ***
Pintail	>27yrs 5mths *	**Turnstone**	>21yrs 5mths **
Oystercatcher	43yrs 4mths ****	**Mediterranean Gull**	17yrs 11mths **
Avocet	27yrs 10mths ‡	**Black-headed Gull**	30yrs 7mths ***
Ringed Plover	>20yrs 9mths **	**Common Gull**	33yrs 8mths ‡
Golden Plover	>12yrs 9mths *	**Lesser Black-backed Gull**	34yrs 11mths ***
Grey Plover	25yrs 7mths ***	**Herring Gull**	34yrs 9mths †
Lapwing	>23yrs 7mths †	**Glaucous Gull**	18yrs 8mths *
Knot	26yrs 8mths **	**Great Black-backed Gull**	27yrs 1mths *
Sanderling	>18yrs 6mths **	**Sandwich Tern**	30yrs 9mths †
Curlew Sandpiper	19yrs 8mths *	**Common Tern**	33yrs ‡
Purple Sandpiper	20yrs 9mths **	**Arctic Tern**	30yrs 11mths ***
Dunlin	28yrs 10mths **	**Little Tern**	23yrs 11mths **
Snipe	>16yrs 3mths *		

* Shot	**** killed by bird of prey
** caught and released again	† killed by human
*** found dead	‡ ring number read in the field

Based on the recovery or control of ringed birds. *Source: Staav, R. & Fransson, T. (2008) EURING list of longevity records for European birds. www.euring.org (http://www.euring.org/data_and_codes/longevity.htm)*

Increased human disturbance on the shore can also have a significant effect on shorebird survival. Something as innocent as letting dogs run around on a beach or strand can result in shorebirds being unable to feed or rest which, in turn, will affect their chances of survival. Shorebird habitat destruction has also played its part, such as the removal of critical feeding and roosting areas. Studies have shown that a sudden loss of habitat at a particular site has a dramatic effect on the long-term survival of the birds that used that habitat.

Iceland - A Shorebird Maternity Unit

Iceland is Europe's youngest country, roughly 25 million years old. Long before Saint Brendan first saw this land of fire and ice, and the Vikings established the first human settlements, shorebirds colonised the vast expanse of wetland habitat. Although well known for its volcanoes and glaciers, Iceland has a climate that suits shorebirds looking for a place to breed. In spite of being of recent volcanic origin, Iceland is typical of most of the breeding grounds of shorebirds that spend the winter in Ireland. It provides plenty of suitable places to build a nest, a large supply of food for hungry chicks and the bonus of almost twenty-four hours of daylight to allow the chicks to develop quickly in the relatively short summer. Ten shorebird species that breed in Iceland spend all or part of the winter in Ireland.

A black-tailed godwit coming into land near its nest in a meadow in northern Iceland.

The Birthplace of Millions of Waders

Each winter thousands of shorebirds come to Ireland from Iceland. Large numbers of wigeon and tufted duck as well as smaller numbers of teal, pintail and lesser black-backed gulls found in Ireland in the winter are from Iceland. But it is Icelandic waders that make up a significant proportion of shorebirds found in Ireland in the winter.

In order to give the reader an insight into the places where our migrant shorebirds go to breed, in this chapter Dr Tómas Grétar Gunnarsson, Director of the University of Iceland's South Iceland Research Centre, tells of the waders that winter in Ireland and breed in Iceland.

Quite a few years ago now, I visited Ireland for the first time. I came to study one of your most beautiful shorebirds, the black-tailed godwit. It was a mid-winter visit, aimed at finding individually marked black-tailed godwits which I had caught with my colleagues in Iceland the preceding summer. We inspected mudflats and grasslands from Wexford in the east to the Shannon in the west and were delighted to find several of our marked godwits. Although our trip was a success in the scientific sense, finding the godwits was not the only highlight of the trip. It was seeing Icelandic shorebirds en masse on the Irish wintering grounds for the first time. It was obviously the place to be. Tens of thousands of golden plovers on mudflats and fields and snipe jumping out of every ditch. Well, I assumed they were Icelandic given the proximity of the countries and the fact that Iceland is the main 'shorebird factory' for many of Europe's winter shorebirds. It has been estimated that over 4 million waders alone leave Iceland in the autumn each year and many of them head for Ireland. And that is excluding the high-Arctic migrant waders that pass through the country going north in spring and south in autumn as well as other shorebirds like ducks, geese and gulls. After much larger Russia, Iceland, which is only roughly the size of Ireland (approximately 101,000 km²), is considered the most productive shorebird country in Europe. On the following pages I will briefly explore the nature of Iceland with the eyes of a shorebird and some of the links Iceland and Ireland share through the movements of these magnificent creatures.

Dr Tómas Grétar Gunnarsson, Director of the University of Iceland's South Iceland Research Centre.

Facing page:
Whimbrel look very like a curlew with a short beak. They breed in Iceland, winter in Africa and stop off on Irish shores during their migration in spring and autumn.

An Island Sculpted by Climate, Volcanoes and Humans

Iceland is a young country in geological terms. It is situated on the Mid-Atlantic Ridge where the Eurasian and the North American tectonic plates meet. Iceland is a hotspot and volcanic activity is high with frequent eruptions and widespread geothermals, especially on a southwest–northeast axis where the Atlantic ridge lies. New material reaches the surface in frequent eruptions and the plates drift apart at a rate of about 1 cm per year. Consequently, the eastern and western parts of the country are oldest, between 3 million and 16 million years old. Land closer to the active belt from southwest to northeast is mostly covered by lava fields from modern times, less than 10,000 years old. The soils of Iceland are largely of volcanic origin, termed Andosols. These soils are fragile but have a high organic content and good water retention properties. Their volcanic nature seems to have beneficial effects on soil creatures like earthworms which constitute a large part of the diet of waders during the breeding season but further research is needed to validate this.

Despite its northerly latitude (between 63° and 66° N), the maritime climate of Iceland has mild winters but relatively cool summers. Annual mean temperature ranges from 2.0 °C to 5.7 °C in lowland areas but is slightly lower in the highlands. A warm current, the Irminger Current (a branch of the North Atlantic Drift) flows from the south and runs along the south, west and north coasts whereas a branch of the cool East Greenland Current flows along the east coast. Precipitation is moderate but wind velocities are often high following frequent passing of low pressure systems. Most of the country is rather high ground with the average being around 500 m above sea level. Lowland areas are prominent in the south and in the west but are otherwise mostly found as small pockets in the innermost parts of fjords around the northwest, north and east coasts. Human settlements and agriculture are limited to the lowland areas.

There is evidence to suggest that Irish monks were the first people to set foot on Icelandic soil in the sixth century AD but it was not until around the tenth century AD that Iceland was evidently colonised by humans and still has the lowest density human population in Europe with only 300,000 people approximately. Molecular genetics have established that about three-quarters of the male settlers were of Norwegian origin whereas more than half of the female settlers were of Gaelic origin, lending some credibility to sagas of Vikings raiding Ireland. This shows that both countries are not only linked

by shorebirds but through human history. Pollen analyses show that during the times of the settlement, Iceland was largely covered in birch forest especially in the highlands, although the exact distribution is unclear. Effects of the settlement on the vegetation of Iceland were abrupt, creating vast expanses of deforested areas both in the lowlands and highlands. The forest was cut for timber and grazed by livestock. The loss of forests rendered the country more vulnerable to volcanic eruptions and the cooling climate of the post-settlement ages resulting in some of the highest levels of desertification in Europe, especially in the interior.

Clockwise from above left:
Active geothermal areas such as geysers and hot springs of mud and water can be found in many parts of Iceland.

The beautiful Icelandic horse can be found all over Iceland.

A surprising number of colourful flowers can be seen in Iceland during their short summer such as this patch of Moss Campion.

Flora and Fauna

The current landscape of Iceland still bears the marks of the catastrophic changes caused by deforestation: open treeless expanses of land, which is, nevertheless, very suitable for shorebirds. In fact, shorebirds have flourished in a large part due to these human-induced changes, since they need open landscapes for their elaborate courtship displays and breeding places. A second wave of human-made changes occurred in the mid-twentieth century when large-scale drainage of wetlands began. During a period of roughly forty years, most of the wetlands of lowland Iceland were drained to a greater or lesser extent under the flag of land improvement for agriculture. Large parts of the lowland areas, especially the plains of the south and the river valleys in the north, are still very wet and are functioning wetlands with wetland vegetation and high densities of breeding shorebirds. Other types of prominent habitat types include heathland, grasslands, sparsely vegetated plains along rivers, and cultivated fields. Agriculture in Iceland is still at a very low level in most areas and is nowhere as intense as in most of western Europe. Most cultivation is for animal fodder, mainly hay and recently barley, as the growing season is too short for most crops. The highlands of Iceland are unvegetated to a large extent. The existing vegetation is found as patches of tundra-like habitats usually fed by large, glacial rivers. Although Iceland is often noted as tundra on global maps, actual permafrost is found only in these isolated pockets in the highlands. Pink-footed geese, long-tailed ducks, scaup, dunlins and purple sandpipers are some of the common

bird species in these highland oases.

An overseas visitor with a keen eye for nature will immediately observe that the diversity of plants and animal species in Iceland is low. During the last ice age (*c.* 10,000 years ago) Iceland was, most likely, totally covered in ice, and colonisation by flora and fauna has taken place only since then. Iceland, being an isolated island in the middle of the north Atlantic, is dominated by species with good dispersal abilities. Of the eighty or so fairly common species of breeding birds, strong flyers or good swimmers dominate, namely, seabirds, wildfowl and waders. Nearly half of all regular breeding species are shorebirds. The number of land bird species, such as thrushes, finches and warblers, is very low compared to elsewhere in Europe with only about ten regular breeding species. There is only one native mammal, the arctic fox, which colonised by travelling over the ice bridge which, for a while, connected Iceland to Greenland after the last ice age. Since the settlement, reindeer, brown rat, black rat, wood mouse, house mouse and recently American mink have been introduced. There are fewer than 400 common species of vascular plants, some widespread but others only common locally. The flora and fauna are largely of European origin and only a few species have come from the west. With the possible exception of one plant species, a realtive of eyebright called *Euphrasia Calida*, there are no species of plants or animals endemic to Iceland.

Slavonian or horned grebe, a stunning Icelandic breeding bird with its chick with the striped head.

The Waders of Iceland

What Iceland lacks in diversity it makes up for in numbers. For example, it has been estimated that about half of the world's population of golden plovers breeds in Iceland and almost 40 per cent of whimbrels (see the table opposite). My great-great grandfather was on a mission to exterminate all snipe from Iceland because his horse shied every time they flew up from underneath. The method he used was to eat every snipe egg he could find. This would have been a very slow process since there are probably over half a million snipe nests in Iceland each spring! In general, the waders are the most visible group of birds in the Icelandic landscape. In a bird survey undertaken around lowland Iceland between 2001 and 2003, 64 per cent of the birds recorded were waders. It would be difficult to find such wader abundance elsewhere in Europe during the breeding season. Although no ongoing monitoring of breeding numbers is carried out in Iceland, most populations seem to be faring well. What makes Iceland good for waders is the open space with suitable habitats and particularly the low intensity land-use by a small human population.

About half a million snipe breed in Iceland each year.

Estimated Icelandic population (i.e., individuals in autumn)

and estimated percentage of the world population for the common breeding waders in Iceland.

Species	Iceland Population	% of world population in Iceland
Oystercatcher	45,000	4
Golden Plover	930,000	52
Ringed Plover	150,000	32
Whimbrel	750,000	40
Dunlin	810,000	16
Purple Sandpiper	90,000	46
Snipe	600,000	6
Redshank	420,000	19
Black-tailed Godwit	71,000	10
Red-necked Phalarope	150,000	6

Waders lead a double life. In winter they flock together and frequent the shoreline. In summer they are hostile towards each other and most defend inland breeding territories. The timing of their arrival and breeding is probably largely determined by resource abundance on the breeding grounds. It is timed so that the period of the peak food requirements of the chicks coincides with the midsummer peak in the

Over half of the world's population of golden plover breed in Iceland.

The red-necked phalarope, a shorebird that is a speciality of Iceland, is different from other waders in that it spends up to nine months a year at sea. Interestingly, it is the female which is brightly coloured while the male is much duller. The red-necked phalarope is rare in Ireland but the species has bred here in the past.

abundance of insects. In Iceland this is near mid-July so successful waders should have large, hungry chicks at that time. To do so they need to breed by mid-May and for that they need to arrive in April, in order not to find themselves outcompeted for territories. Indeed, most of the waders reach Iceland in April, although many oystercatchers and a few individuals of other species arrive in late March. Individual waders are each on their own schedule, which is probably due to local adaptation to a particular breeding place to which they mostly remain faithful throughout their usually long lives. These individual migratory schedules are so finely tuned that in pairs of black-tailed godwits that winter separately in western Europe, males and females usually arrive within two days of each other on the breeding territory of the previous year. If they fail to do so, divorce can be imminent as there is no time to waste!

The autumn migration is more relaxed and less synchronised across the population. Birds that fail in their attempts to breed start leaving for western Europe by June, but adults that succeed mostly leave Iceland between mid-July and mid-August. The juveniles born that year, however, leave the country on average two to three weeks later than the adults and, admirably, manage to find the wintering grounds by themselves. Most Icelandic waders winter in western Europe, mainly in Ireland, the UK, France and Portugal. A few species

go all the way to West Africa, such as ringed plover, whimbrel and dunlin. Few waders winter in Iceland except for a few thousand oystercatchers and purple sandpipers, along with smaller numbers of redshank and turnstone.

During the spring and summer, wetlands of various types are the best places to see breeding waders. Most of the waders show some preference for marshes, bogs, river plains and wet features like pools and streams. Studies of the habitat selection of black-tailed godwits within individual breeding sites show that while the adults prefer wet features and place their nests in the marshes, the chicks do most of their feeding in adjacent drier grasslands and meadows where more food (such as insects) is available. This shows that habitat selection of birds can be more complex than is immediately obvious and different life stages often have different requirements. Recent studies show that across the country the density of waders varies considerably. Wetlands in the south and north of Iceland have three to four times higher densities than wetlands in the east and west. Perhaps this pattern is partly explained by volcanic activity but hydrology is also likely to play a role.

Detailed international collaborative studies, on the population of black-tailed godwits that breed in Iceland and spend the winter along west European shores and wetlands from Ireland to Portugal,

Above from left:

Over half a million Dunlin breed in Iceland and pass through Ireland on their way to and from their wintering grounds mainly in west Africa

The Arctic skua, closely related to the gull family, preys on shorebird chicks and eggs.

The lowlands of south Iceland, prime breeding habitat for the black-tailed godwit.

have revealed some remarkable links between countries. The godwit population has increased manyfold in recent decades. During this increase the population has been expanding into poorer quality godwit habitat areas in both winter and summer. In winter this means that they have colonised areas where food abundance and survival are lower, and in summer they are found in areas where breeding success is lower. By tracking individual godwits (with a diagnostic combination of colour rings on the legs) it has been shown that it is the same individuals that occupy either higher quality habitats in both winter and summer, or poorer quality habitats in winter and summer. This has very important and varied consequences for population dynamics. For example, it means that as the same individuals are more likely both to survive and reproduce, so conserving the networks of sites that these individuals use becomes more critical for the godwits to survive in the future.

So how do we know whether our site holds 'high–quality' individuals or not? In most cases we don't know, as this pattern has been quantified only for a particular population of godwits, although we suspect that it might be a general phenomenon for most migrants. It stands to reason that, within seasons, 'good' birds tend to occupy good sites. But there are some observations that are likely to apply to shorebirds in general. To begin with, large sites are usually better, partly because they more often contain a mosaic of patches that can have favourable feeding conditions at different times, whereas birds wintering at a small site have few, if any, alternatives if the feeding conditions fail. In fact, most of the originally (pre-1960) occupied godwit sites were large estuarine complexes with many bays, creeks, good roost sites and even adjacent grassland that also had good feeding grounds. The Tagus Estuary in Portugal, Bay de l'Aguillion in France, the Solent in England and Cork Harbour in Ireland are beautiful examples of world-class shorebird sites. Other top-notch sites in Ireland include the Shannon Estuary, the Little Brosna Callows and Dublin Bay.

During the spring and autumn, hundreds of thousands of migrant waders pass through Iceland on their way to and from their high-Arctic breeding grounds in Greenland and Canada. They peak in numbers on shores in the latter part of May. Knot, turnstone and sanderling are most obvious. Populations of ringed plovers, dunlins and purple sandpipers also pass through, but these three species mix with local breeding populations so can be difficult to tell apart. The west coast of Iceland is the best place for these passage migrants to be since the shoreline is very intricate and accounts for over 70 per cent of the total length of the Icelandic shoreline.

Future of Iceland's shorebirds

The future of Icelandic shorebirds depends largely upon the action of humans. The more suitable habitat in good condition there is, the safer the future of the shorebirds. For the waders of Iceland their existence will depend mostly on land-use patterns in lowland areas. Low intensity agriculture, open, treeless landscape and low-level industry are favourable for waders. The shoreline of Iceland is long and is mostly undamaged by human activity. The birds breeding and wintering there are largely dependent on oceanic conditions. These include both large-scale phenomena under the influence of global change and smaller-scale events such as the effects of harvesting on food stocks. Hopefully, we will have the good sense to treat the shorebirds and their environment with the respect they deserve, assuring the steady flow of shorebirds from Iceland to Ireland each autumn. And, of course, we also hope that they will be treated well on the shores of Ireland so we can enjoy them again in spring.

Tómas Grétar Gunnarsson

Studying Shorebirds

Below from left:

Engraved 'darvic' coloured rings have been used very successfully on gulls such as this black-headed gull. The bird was ringed as a chick in Gloucestershire, England, and photographed at the Lough in Cork city six months later.

Brent goose 'yellow U lime F'. The colours and letters can be clearly read from a distance.

This Brent goose was ringed at Hvalfjörður in southwest Iceland in May 2005 and was seen at Strangford Lough, County Down, in October, then in Dublin Bay the following March and back in Hvalfjörður in May. It was back in Strangford Lough in October before being photographed in Dublin Bay in November 2008.

How have we come to know so much about shorebirds when individuals of a species all look the same to us and often fly thousands of kilometres a year spending lots of time in very remote parts of the world, we can be fairly sure that from the first time human beings noticed the appearance and disappearance of birds through the seasons we wondered where they went. Aristotle, the famous Greek philosopher knew from observations that cranes migrated from the steppes of Scythia, east of Greece, to the marshes of the Nile. Unfortunately he also tried to explain the disappearance and reappearance of birds by suggesting that they hibernated or transformed into different types of birds. In the early eighteenth century one writer suggested they went to the moon! Even in the nineteenth century, in some parts, it was believed that swallows spent the winter underwater, at the bottom of reed stems along rivers, bogs and lakes. For us today these ideas seem foolish but without the development of a system for tracking birds, their movements might still be a mystery and hibernation and moon migration might not seem so silly at all.

It was the development of systematic tagging of birds at the very end of the nineteenth century that finally opened the door to the astonishing world of bird migration and behaviour. The system, largely unchanged, is still in use today and involves placing a very

light metal alloy ring around the leg of a bird. On this ring is stamped a unique number or combination of letters and numbers and an address. This is known as 'bird ringing' (in the USA it is called 'bird banding'). The person who puts the ring on the bird's leg is called a 'ringer'.

Before you can put a ring on a shorebird, first you have to catch it: it is not an easy task since a bird that lives out in the open is very wary and you cannot get close to it without being seen. A variety of methods is used today, many adapted from old bird hunting techniques. The most commonly used method is to catch the bird using what is called a mist net. This is a net made of fine cord which is strung out between tall poles. Mist netting shorebirds is usually carried out at night where the birds come to roost at high tide. Birds cannot see the nets in the dark and get caught as they fly in to land. Birds can also be ringed as chicks before they fledge. Other methods are also used such as cannon netting in which a net is fired over a flock of shorebirds on the ground, or by using what is called a 'walk-in' trap, using the principle of the lobster pot, when the bird walks in, it cannot find its way out and so can be caught and ringed. Ducks have been successfully caught using very large funnel traps. Once caught, a trained bird ringer then carefully removes the bird from the net or trap and places the uniquely numbered metal ring on one of its legs.

When a bird is caught for ringing a lot of valuable information is recorded such as weight, length of various parts of the bird, the

Below from left:
A bird ringer is highly trained to ensure the birds caught come to no harm.

Special safety pliers are used to put a metal ring on a wader's leg.

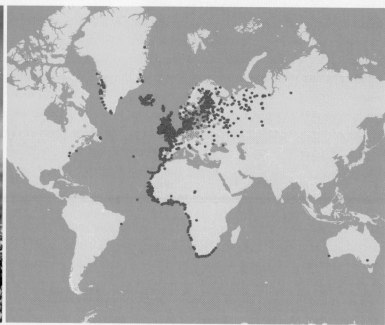

Above from left:

This godwit was colour-ringed by Þorlákur Sigurbjörnsson on his farm in northern Iceland and has been seen in Ireland, France and England.

This remarkable map shows all the places where shorebirds ringed in Ireland (blue dots) have been found or seen again and all places abroad (yellow dots) where shorebirds have been ringed and found or seen in Ireland. (Courtesy of the British Trust for Ornithology)

condition of the feathers and, if moulting, what stage it is at. A rough idea of the amount of fat the bird is carrying can also be measured, as can the amount of muscle. All this information has proved to be invaluable in the study of shorebirds. The bird ringer then releases the ringed bird unharmed and waits to see if anyone will catch or find it and send back the unique number to her or him, along with any details of when and where it was found. In ringing terms, if the ringed bird is caught again, the ring details recorded and the bird released once more it is referred to as a control, if it is found dead it is referred to as a recovery. Some people think bird ringing is cruel. However, this is not the case as the birds are not harmed and the information gathered has helped us to understand the needs of shorebirds, which in turn has allowed us to protect the lives of far more birds than those caught for ringing and has provided invaluable information that will help us protect them and their environment for the future.

Tens of thousands of shorebirds are ringed in this way every year and, despite the fact that the recovery/control rate is very low and that the smaller the bird the smaller the recovery/control rate, over the last 100 years a very complicated picture has emerged of the movements and behaviour of our shorebirds using this simple method of study. Many shorebirds such as teal and curlew are hunted in Europe and beyond. As a result the recovery rates for these may be as high as 10 to 15 per cent, whereas for the smaller shorebirds such as dunlin the recovery rate may be as low as 1 per cent or less. As bird ringing

became the tool of choice for studying shorebirds, its limitations soon began to emerge. For example, you only get information on the bird you ringed if it is caught again or someone finds it dead and notices the ring. You then have to rely on the person finding 'your' bird to go to the trouble of taking down the information on the ring accurately and sending that information back to you. Without having the bird in your hand, apart from large shorebirds such as geese, the chances of reading the information on the ring is almost impossible without catching the bird. For example the ring on a dunlin, a bird the size of a starling, is only 7 mm tall and the letters are just 2 mm tall. You also know very little about the details of the birds movements. Most birds would be found dead so you only know where it was ringed and where it died, but nothing about its travels in between. Some researchers started putting harmless dye on shorebirds that could be seen from a distance. This helped to work out if they were looking at the same individuals all the time or if some birds were leaving the area and other undyed birds taking their place. They could also watch their movements over short distances. This method of study is only of short-term use because, once the birds moult their feathers, the harmless dye disappears.

Other researchers then started putting unique combinations of very lightwight, coloured, plastic rings on birds which allowed the individual birds to be identified from a distance without having to catch them. This method has become very popular with shorebird

Even at a distance this colour-ringed knot stands out from the rest of the roosting flock in Dublin Bay in December 2008. It was caught and colour-ringed in De Richel, north Netherlands, in October 2005.

researchers because most shorebirds have relatively long legs, are fairly big and spend a lot of time in the open where their legs can be clearly seen. With the advent of high-power, affordable binoculars, telescopes and digital cameras this technique has proved to be invaluable in unravelling the mysteries of shorebird movements. Colour-ringing schemes have been used to study almost every shorebird species.

An excellent example of the value of this method of studying birds is that of the international study of the Icelandic black-tailed godwit. This international project, known as Operation Godwit, began in 1992 and since then about 3,000 of these long-legged shorebirds have been caught and given a unique combination of coloured plastic rings. Proof that these rings do not cause any harm to the birds is that there are many alive and well five, ten and even sixteen years after they were colour-ringed.

Amateur and professional ornithologists as well as members of the public have tracked the movements of these birds across Western Europe and beyond. Since the start of the scheme about 60,000 sightings of the colour-ringed godwits have been recorded.

Analysis of these valuable sightings has revealed some remarkable facts about the lives of these godwits. One amazing finding has been that male and female Icelandic black-tailed godwits spend the winter in different parts of Europe, as much as 1,000 kilometres apart, and

Below, clockwise from top left:

This godwit was ringed in Portugal in November 2008 and has stopped off at Harper's Island in Cork en route to its breeding grounds in Iceland.

Locations where nine colour-ringed black-tailed godwits present in a flock of 1,700 Icelandic black-tailed godwit on 16 April 2009 at Harper's Island, Cork Harbour, have been seen in the past.

This godwit was ringed in Kent, England.

Source: Operation Godwit Data courtesy of Tómas Gunnarsson/ Pete Potts/José Alves.

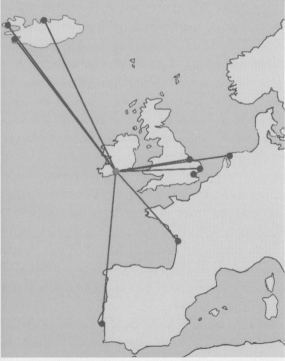

return, without meeting up along the way, to the same nesting site each year, often arriving within two or three days of each other. It has also been discovered that if their partner from last year is late, she or he will not wait around for long and will seek a new mate.

Birds travelling from their breeding areas in temperate latitudes to wintering grounds in the tropics, or even farther, often cover thousands of kilometres each way. Because of ringing studies we know that the absolute record-breaker is the Arctic tern (*Sterna paradisaea*), which flies a phenomenal round-trip of approximately 32,000 kilometres per year, from the Arctic to the Antarctic and back.

Advances in micro-electronic technology in recent years has meant that other methods of studying the movements of shorebirds have emerged. The best known of these is satellite tracking. This involves placing a small satellite transmitter on the back of a bird and tracking its movements via satellite. Unlike the colour rings which rely on the individual bird being spotted and the full combination recorded, with a satellite tag it is possible to follow every movement of the bird without physically seeing it. The tags are still quite expensive so are not widely used. Bar-tailed godwits (*Limosa lapponica*) that breed in western Alaska winter in New Zealand and Australia on the other side of the Pacific Ocean. In 2007 one female bar-tailed godwit called 'E7' was fitted with a tiny temporary satellite transmitter in Alaska and to the amazement of the researchers they discovered that she flew the 11,600-kilometre journey non-stop in just nine days.

Brent geese have been satellite tagged in Ireland. The tags are light and not permanent, and fall off the bird within a few months. The size of these transmitters is getting smaller by the day and soon it will be possible to fit one on most shorebirds. The problem for those who started ringing birds just over 100 years ago was having so little

Below from left:
The map shows the route taken by two brent geese that were satellite tagged in Wexford on 1 April 2005. The satellite information received from the tagged geese showed that the journey to Iceland for one of the birds commenced on 16 April 2005 and moved gradually up the Irish east coast. That bird left Ireland one evening and the flight to Iceland took about twenty-four hours. The birds then rested and fattened up for six weeks in western Iceland and arrived at their breeding grounds in high-Arctic Canada in fewer than five days. Both returned to Wexford the following winter.
Map courtesy of Kendrew Colhoun and Dr Gudmundur Gudmundsson.

Watching and studying shorebirds can become a very rewarding lifelong hobby or career.

data to analyse: the problem for the ornithologists in the future will be how to deal with so much.

Studying birds by ringing them requires specialist equipment, training and a government licence and requires a lot of time and dedication. One important method of gathering information on shorebirds, which anyone can do, is by observing them, recording their numbers, their appearance and behaviour. If this is carried out in a systematic way over a long period of time, a lot of valuable information can be gathered. Before systematic methods of studying shorebirds were developed, most of our knowledge had come from hunters whose very existence depended on knowing the haunts and behaviour of these birds and some were exceptional ornithologists. In Ireland, BirdWatch Ireland, the Royal Society for the Protection of Birds (RSPB) and the British Trust for Ornithology (BTO) have being carrying out systematic studies for many years. The first systematic counts of shorebirds in Ireland were carried out in the late 1940s and early 1950s and, since then, various national and international surveys have been performed. Currently in the Republic, BirdWatch Ireland is undertaking a long-term study of our wetland birds, many of which are shorebirds, called the Irish Wetland Bird Survey (I-WeBS). Every year, the I-WeBS data are combined with those from other countries around the world as part of the International Waterbird Census, organised by Wetlands International, to report at an international level on waterbird populations. I-WeBS is a joint project of the National Parks and Wildlife Service and BirdWatch Ireland. In Northern Ireland, the Wetland Bird Survey (WEBS) is jointly run by the BTO, WWT (Wildfowl & Wetland Trust) and RSPB. It is a survey that was initiated in the winter of 1994/'95, with the aim of monitoring all non-breeding waterbirds including shorebirds that spend the winter in Ireland. Every winter, Ireland, north and south, is required to make special provision for wetlands and wetland birds (EU Birds Directive, Ramsar Convention, African-Eurasian Waterbird Agreement, Wetlands International). Wild birds and their habitats are protected through national and European legislation, as well as through international agreements and conventions. Ireland is legally and morally obliged to protect these waterbirds and the wetlands that they use.

I-WeBS has three main aims:
- To assess the importance of individual sites for waterbirds
- To assess the size of non-breeding waterbird populations in Ireland
- To assess trends in their numbers and distribution

To this end, I-WeBS waterbird counts are carried out at wetlands across the island of Ireland by hundreds of skilled volunteer observers and professional ornithologists. The efforts and skills of these observers form the most important component of the survey. The counts are made annually once a month from September to March at all types of wetlands, including salt marshes, open coast, estuaries, and also on adjacent lands where some birds may be feeding. The long-term data that are obtained are used extensively by the Irish and UK governments to fulfil their international conservation obligations, one of which is to identify sites worthy of designation in the EU-wide network of Special Protection Areas. The information gathered also regularly contributes to informed decision-making by planners, developers and conservation bodies in Ireland.

The purpose of all these studies is to allow us to build up a picture of the needs of these incredible birds. Without all the hours of hard work and dedication of thousands of amateur and professional ornithologists, we would know nothing about our shorebirds and the places where they live. We would not know where the most important places are for them and what we need to do to preserve this invaluable part of our natural heritage. Another important use of the study of shorebirds is to detect changes in our environment. Shorebirds are very sensitive to such changes and long-term monitoring can give us early warning signals of environmental changes that might affect our lives.

Top ten Irish internationally* important sites for shorebirds (2002–2007)

	2002/03	2003/04	2004/05	2005/06	2006/07	Mean
Dundalk Bay	47,042	66,309	53,004	55,986	62,536	56,975
Wexford Harbour & Slobs	51,459	49,693	48,487	42,208	–	47,962
Lough Foyle	34,154	37,292	33,076	38,324	34,850	35,530
Dublin Bay	34,996	28,051	27,472	27,536	33,826	30,376
Shannon & Fergus Estuary	13,298	43,611	35,165	25,986	6,990**	29,515
Cork Harbour	29,551	30,368	31,175	26,923	19,669**	29,504
Tralee Bay, Lough Gill & Akeragh Lough	23,758**	23,361**	26,287	29,701	29,142	28,377
Lough Swilly	23,960	26,934	25,213	31,469	31,867	27,889
Rogerstown Estuary	15,908	22,549	21,040	32,339	20,039	22,375
Inner Galway Bay	24,607	17,312	24,870	27,180	14,386	21,671
Ballymacoda (Cork)	20,725	21,033	–	–	–	20,671

*A site is considered internationally important if it holds more than 20,000 waterbirds and/or if it supports at least 1 per cent of the flyway population of any waterbird species. Almost all birds at the sites above are shorebirds.

** Indicates that the counts were incomplete.

The Birds

The following pages describe the main shorebird species, starting with the waders and herons, those carnivorous long-legged birds that have become specialist hunters of the intertidal area. This is followed by the ducks, geese and swans, which are mainly vegetarian and are seen away from the seashore more often than the waders and herons. Then come the gulls and terns, which are usually classified as seabirds but some spend time on the seashore; and finally, the honorary shorebirds, a collection of birds usually classified as 'land birds' but which are seen on the shore regularly or at certain times of the year.

The species maps provide the reader with a general picture of the range of each shorebird species. The extent of the global range of these birds is often greater than that shown on the map but these maps only show the approximate geographical limits of those found on our

Oystercatchers, knot and
bar-tailed godwits crowd a

shores. **Breeding grounds are shown in orange, wintering grounds in blue and where they are found all year round in red**. Birds are also seen in places between their breeding and wintering grounds but, for clarity, these areas are not highlighted. The maps are based primarily on Wetlands International data and a number of other published sources acknowledged in the bibliography.

A measurement grid is provided for each bird. Length is measured from tip of bill to end of tail when stretched out. Wingspan is measured from one wing tip to the other. Weight is in grammes and M (male) & F (female) are given if there is noticeable differences between the sexes. All measurements are average, and not maximum or minimum.

Breeding grounds

Wintering grounds

All year round

SPECIES MAPS - key

Waders and Herons

There are over 210 species worldwide and over 70 species have been recorded in Ireland.

Up until the late 1980s and early 1990s, the little egret was a rare sight on Ireland's shores. Now a common sight on most shorelines around Ireland, it has become a well-established breeding species here.

Oystercatcher *Roilleach*
Haematopus ostralegus

Length	Wingspan	Weight	Oldest-known bird
40–50 cm	80–86 cm	540 g	43 years

One of the easiest shorebirds to recognise with its black-and-white plumage; stout pink legs; long, straight, orange-red beak, red eye and indistinct white half-collar in winter. Young birds have a yellow-orange bill with a dark tip, becoming the colour of an adult as they mature and have a broad white half-collar until they are two or three years old. In flight black-and-white-striped wings and a white triangle on the back are clearly visible and the tail is white with a black band on the end. One good word to describe a group of oystercatchers in flight is a squadron, as their habit of flying rapidly in straight lines or in V-formation, often very low, has a military discipline about it.

The oystercatcher makes a very loud, single-noted piping call, repeated often and sometimes speeding up at the end. Noisy piping sessions can be heard when two or more birds come together, with necks stretched outward and upward and beaks pointing towards the ground. This behaviour is thought to establish the pecking order between the birds involved.

The oystercatcher can live for over forty-two years. Its common Irish name is *roilleach* but has also been called a *scaladóir*, referring to its high, loud call, and *gobadán*, a term used to describe any wader with a long beak. Another name that has been used to describe this bird in Ireland is the 'mussel picker'.

It breeds along our coastline in a variety of coastal habitats, though almost absent from the south coast west of Dungarvan. Small

Facing page:
An adult oystercatcher, one of the easiest shorebirds to identify.

Below:
A squadron of oystercatchers coming in to land on a ebbing tide.

numbers also nest inland. About 4,000 pairs were found breeding in Ireland during the Breeding Atlas Survey (1988–1991). The oystercatcher is unusual amongst waders in that it continues to feed its young for some time after they have fledged. Most oystercatchers born in Ireland stay here, will not breed until at least three to five years old, and many return to the area where they were born to breed. In winter Irish birds are joined by oystercatchers from Iceland and the Faeroes. Mainland European oystercatchers rarely come to Ireland. Flocks of over a hundred are not uncommon. It is very territorial when nesting and during the winter. When feeding it will often chase off other birds while searching for shellfish and worms on mudflats, sandy shores, rocky shores and grassy fields, with a particular fondness for sports fields. Its main prey on the shore is cockles and mussels. Many return to the same wintering areas year after year. The young oystercatcher will wander in the first few years until it becomes sexually mature.

On Irish shores, most are found in estuaries. It has been shown that monitoring the health of oystercatcher populations reflects the health of the estuaries where they winter. Where land-based commercial harvesting of shellfish, especially cockles, takes place, the oystercatcher is sometimes looked on as an enemy, although studies in places where they have been culled have shown that killing them did not have a significant impact on the shellfish population, especially if the minimum cockle size for harvesting is not set too low. Up to 70,000 oystercatchers are found in Ireland in winter and highest concentrations have been recorded in Dundalk Bay (Louth), Strangford Lough (Down) and Belfast Lough.

Below from left:

A flock of oystercatchers heading to roost at high tide.

Unlike us, shorebirds, like the oystercatcher, have to be on constant lookout for danger, even when resting.

Ringed Plover *Feadóg an Fháinne*
Charadrius hiaticula

Length	Wingspan	Weight	Oldest known bird
18–20 cm	48–57 cm	64 g	20 years

The ringed plover, now being referred to globally as the greater ringed plover, is a small wader not much bigger than a robin. The adult has a distinctive head and breast pattern. In the breeding season the forehead is white, surrounded by a black face mask, white eyebrow and a continuous white neck collar. It has a black breast band. The body is dark sandy-brown above and white below. The beak is short and stubby, orange with a black tip and the legs, which are relatively short, are pale orange-red. In winter immature birds and adults have an all-dark bill, olive-grey legs and an incomplete breast band. In flight a white wing bar and white edge to dark tail are visible.

Its call is a loud clear, soft *twoo-ip*, sometimes repeated with descending pitch. Its song includes a rapid, muted *ti-wou*, repeated many times for several seconds and lowering in pitch towards the end.

The ringed plover can live for over twenty years. Two of its Irish names are *Feadóg an Fháinne* and *Feadóg Chladaigh* referring to its flute- or tin-whistle-like call. Another name that has been used to

A juvenile ringed plover with the white neck ring from which it gets its name.

describe this bird in Ireland is the 'bull's eye'. This small plover breeds mainly around our coast, with small numbers breeding on western lakes. An estimated 1,250 pairs were found breeding in Ireland during the Breeding Atlas Survey (1988–1991). As a breeding bird, it is more common north of a line from Dublin to Limerick. It prefers to nest just above the high-water line on shingle or sandy beaches. Increased human disturbance, i.e. many people walking beaches during the breeding season, has led to a decline in recent years. The presence of a breeding pair is easy to prove as the adults are very noisy and pretend to have a broken wing to lure you away from the well-camouflaged eggs. Once you have been drawn far enough away by its very convincing performance, it simply flies off, leaving you far away from its nest. The young are able to leave the nest almost immediately and are equally difficult to locate. Ringed plovers have been shown to be site-faithful with up to 80 per cent returning to the same breeding area each year. From early autumn, flocks of up to 250 birds can be counted on sandy beaches and in some estuaries. They are rarely seen on rocky shores or where mud is too soft. Ringed plovers from Britain, the Baltic, Iceland, Greenland and northern Russia join our own at various times throughout autumn and winter.

The ringed plover feeds mainly on worms and crustaceans. Like many of the plovers it usually feeds by sight and can be seen standing still for a time before dashing forward to inspect the mud or sand closely or to grab an unsuspecting worm. At times it also feeds at night. Many ringed plovers from Canada, Greenland and Scandinavia using the East Atlantic Flyway stop off in Ireland, particularly on the east coast, on their way to wintering grounds farther south in places like Spain and west Africa. Ireland is, therefore, very important for this bird. Up to 15,000 are found in Ireland in winter and highest concentrations have been recorded in Mayo (the Mullet Peninsula, Broadhaven and Blacksod Bays), Down (Outer Ards) and in Kerry (Tralee Bay, Lough Gill and Akeragh Lough).

Facing page, clockwise from top:
An adult ringed plover on a shingle beach.
An orange-beaked adult ringed plover, second from the left, with four dark-beaked juveniles.
 A ringed plover in flight.

Golden Plover *Feadóg Bhuí*
Pluvialis apricaria

Length	Wingspan	Weight	Oldest-known bird
27–29 cm	71–72 cm	220 g	12 years

This beautiful wader gets its name from the golden yellow patches on the feathers of its back and wings. Slightly bigger than a blackbird, it stands very erect. In breeding plumage its face, breast and belly are jet black with a white border separating it from the yellow, black and white speckled cap, back and wings. The black beak is relatively short and thin, the legs relatively long and dark and the large, dark eye is noticeable. In winter the black plumage of the underside is replaced by buff with light-grey streaking, and a pale belly. In flight it looks generally dark above with noticeable white underwings. This contrast between the upper and underwing colours is best seen when a large flock flies in a tight group over an estuary or sandy beach where they move in unison, flashing pale and dark as they 'wheel'. The golden plover's call is a weak-sounding, piping *purr-wee*; the song is more elaborate and generally higher pitched.

The golden plover can live for over twelve years. Its Irish name *Feadóg Bhuí* literally means the 'yellow whistle', the yellow referring to its plumage and the whistle referring to its whistle-like call. Another Irish name, the *Feadóg Shléibhe*, refers to its upland breeding habitat. Other names used to describe this bird in Ireland include black-breasted plover and grey plover. Fewer than 500 pairs breed in Ireland, mainly on blanket and cut-away bogs and almost all on the west coast between Galway and Derry. In winter, Ireland is hugely important for this upland-nesting plover. Adults move south a month or more before the young leave the breeding grounds. Our wintering birds mainly come from Iceland. It is interesting to note that birds born in Britain and Scandinavia are not usually found in Ireland in winter. Ireland is of particular importance for Icelandic-breeding golden plovers.

The golden plover gathers in flocks on large, open, intertidal areas to roost and also spends a lot of time flying in tight or well-scattered flocks, sometimes at great heights. When flying in a scattered flock a distinct edge is often formed by birds flying close in line. At times they will also fly in V-formation. When not roosting on an estuary or sandy beach, golden plover are associated with old pasture fields with lots of earthworms. Some would argue that it is not really a shorebird as it spends most of its time away from the shore, but a large flock

Facing page:
A golden plover displays its cloak of gold sequins in the morning sun.

Rarely seen alone, golden plover sometimes form large flocks in the winter

of these beautiful birds flying over a beach or mudflat at low tide is a memorable sight. Up to 150,000 are found in Ireland in winter and highest concentrations have been recorded in Ballymacoda (Cork), Little Brosna Callows (Tipperary/Offaly border) and Strangford Lough (Down).

Grey Plover *Feadóg Ghlas*
Pluvialis squatarola

Length	Wingspan	Weight	Oldest-known bird
28 cm	76–78 cm	240 g	25 years

As its name suggests and unlike its close relative the golden plover, the grey plover lacks the yellow plumage colours and looks monochrome. In breeding plumage it, too, has a black face, breast and belly, a white cap and chequered black-and-white plumage on the back and wings. In winter it is generally blotchy-grey above and very pale grey below. Its black beak is relatively short and thick and its dark-grey legs are relatively long. In flight, as hinted by its name, it looks grey but it has distinctive black patches at the base of the underwing (like hairy armpits). Its call, heard on the ground or in flight, is a drawn-out, fairly high pitched *que-eeeee* starting on one note dipping to a lower one in the middle and then up to a higher note at the end.

About the size of a blackbird, the grey plover can live for over twenty-five years. Its Irish name, *Feadóg Ghlas*, means the 'grey whistle'. Other names used to describe this bird in Ireland include the strand plover and rock plover. The grey plover breeds in high-Arctic Russia and North America and winters over a large part of temperate and subtropical areas and is considered one of the most

Grey plover hunt alone and will often be seen with other shorebirds such as these dunlin.

globally widespread of the waders. Grey plovers found in Ireland in the winter breed in northern Russia. Ireland is one of the most northerly wintering grounds for this bird.

Unlike the golden plover, the grey plover is mainly a coastal shorebird, preferring estuaries and sandy beaches and spending almost all its time there. It feeds mainly on small shellfish and a variety of marine worms. Like many of the plovers, it usually feeds by sight and can be seen standing still for a time before dashing forward to inspect the mud or sand closely or to grab an unsuspecting worm. It regularly feeds at night. It is faithful to a particular feeding area on a mudflat and will return to the same area year after year. It appears to be more common towards the south and east. It is very vulnerable to severely cold weather. Up to 7,500 are found in Ireland each in winter and highest concentrations have been recorded at Wexford Harbour and Slobs, Dublin Bay and Ballymacoda (Cork).

Left: A grey plover on the lookout for its next meal.

Lapwing *Pilibín*
Vanellus vanellus

Length	Wingspan	Weight	Oldest-known bird
28–31 cm	70–76 cm	230 g	23 years

The lapwing is the only Irish wader with a long, thin crest, longer on the male than the female or young birds. It has a complex black-and-white face pattern, black breast, white belly and a chestnut patch under the tail. The wings are broad, round and black, apart from small, white patches on the outer four wing feathers. It has iridescent blue and green on wings and back, reminiscent of a magpie. The tail is white with a black band on the end. Its black beak is short, straight and stubby, and its pink-red legs are long. In flight, at a distance, a flock of lapwing 'twinkles' as the white belly is revealed and obscured by the dark wings. Its unmistakeable call is usually an eerie, squeaky sound or, as another of its names suggests, a squeaky *peewit*, sounding not unlike a squeaky rubber duck. Its song is similar in sound to the call but a bit more elaborate.

The lapwing can live for over twenty-three years. Its most common Irish name, *Pilibín,* is sometimes used as a general term for a plover

When severe winter weather hits continental Europe thousands of lapwing fly to Ireland for refuge.

and literally means 'little Philip'. The origin of this is unclear and may be a corruption of another Irish word or a phonetic word for the sound of its call. Other names used to describe this bird in Ireland include peewit, green plover and phillipene. The acrobatic display flights and calls of the lapwing during the breeding season are spectacular. In Ireland, it breeds mainly in the midlands and north. About 21,500 pairs were found breeding in Ireland during the Breeding Atlas Survey (1988–1991). A serious decline in breeding birds in the last twenty-five years is largely owing to changes in agricultural practices, where drainage and intermixed grasslands have led to a decline in suitable breeding habitat.

In winter the lapwing is our most widespread wader, with flocks turning up anywhere, though usually not far from wetland areas. Irish birds are joined by birds mainly from northern Britain, and in very cold weather also by lapwing from continental Europe. Flocks of up to 10,000 can sometimes be seen. The lapwing feeds on invertebrates and has a preference for ploughed fields, though in cold weather when the ground freezes it moves to estuaries, where it feeds on worms and small invertebrates. Like many of the plovers it usually feeds by sight and can be seen standing still for a time before moving forward to inspect the mud or sand closely or to grab an unsuspecting worm. It regularly feeds at night. While most lapwing return to the area where they were born to breed there is evidence to show that some undergo what is called abmigration, with birds born in Britain and Ireland joining flocks from abroad and turning up as breeding birds as far away as Russia. This could occur during cold weather movements when young birds from Ireland get caught up in flocks of east European birds and fly back with them once the cold spell is over. Up to 200,000 are found in Ireland in the winter and highest concentrations have been recorded at Shannon and Fergus Estuaries, Shannon Callows and Wexford Harbour and Slobs.

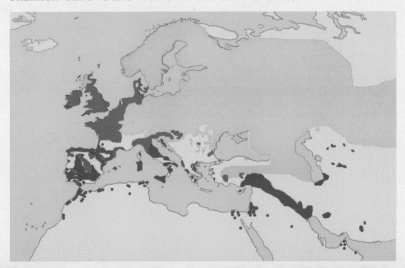

Knot *Cnota*
Calidris canutus

Length	Wingspan	Weight	Oldest-known bird
23–25 cm	58–60 cm	140 g	26 years

In recent times the knot is also referred to as the red knot. The knot is about the size of a blackbird. In winter plumage, this plump, light-grey wader with short olive-coloured legs and a short, slightly curved, dark beak looks pale grey at a distance but up close looks scaled on the back and wings. The underside is pale with grey streaking on the breast and flanks. The wing tips are dark, the rump is barred and the tail grey. In summer plumage, the face, breast and belly become rusty red, from which it gets its English name. There are also flecks of rusty red on the back and wings. When seen from above in flight a thin, white wing stripe is visible on the open wing, broadening out towards the wing tips. It is usually seen in flocks and flies with rapid wingbeats. The call is a high-pitched *whick-whick-whick* often repeated over and over and also a lower pitched *knuuutt* sound.

The knot can live for over twenty-six years. The Irish name is a Gaelicised version of the English name which refers to its call. Other names used to describe this bird in Ireland include red sandpiper and sea snipe.

The knot makes some of the longest non-stop migrations of any wader. A true shorebird, it is rarely seen away from estuaries and bays. A number of subspecies are recognised and almost all of those found in Ireland are of the *islandica* race. *Islandica* knot, which either winter in Ireland or pass through in autumn and spring, breed in northern Greenland and in high-Arctic Canada. Some fly up to 5,000 kilometres between breeding and wintering grounds in Ireland and Western Europe with few stops. Many coming from wintering sites farther south stop off here in the spring to put on fat before flying north to their next refuelling stop in western Iceland or possibly northern Norway, before finally returning to the breeding grounds. The knot acquires its stunning red breeding plumage in the spring by undergoing a moult of body feathers only. There is evidence to show that we sometimes see knot of the *canutus* race, which breeds in Siberia and winters in west and southern Africa. These knot fly over 15,000 kilometres between their breeding and wintering grounds. The male usually does most of the chick-rearing once they are hatched. The female leaves the breeding grounds first, followed by the male once the young are fledged, and then followed

Facing page:
Long-distance migrants, from Siberia pass through Ireland on the way to South Africa for the winter.

On the march, a rising tide herds these knot up the beach.

by juveniles. All stop off for two to three weeks in western Iceland to put on fat before flying on to Western Europe where they undergo a full moult of their feathers.

The knot moves between estuaries, but for most of the winter it uses sites to which it returns to year after year. It prefers mudflats but can occasionally be found on rocky shores. It feeds mainly on invertebrates, with a preference for small shellfish especially Baltic tellin or Baltic macoma (*Macoma balthica*) and also laver spire shell (*Hydrobia ulvae*) and others. Because of its specialised diet and highly migratory habits, the knot is very susceptible to climate and habitat change as it often requires a good supply of food to put on fat quickly before its long-distance migrations. It is found in relatively large concentrations at a few sites during the winter and on migration. Because of this, researchers consider that knot could suffer a sharp decline in population should these few sites be damaged by human activity or lost through global warming. Up to 34,000 are found here in winter and highest concentrations have been recorded at Dundalk Bay (Louth), Strangford Lough (Down) and Dublin Bay.

Sanderling *Luathrán*
Calidris alba

Length	Wingspan	Weight	Oldest-known bird
20–21 cm	41–43 cm	59 g	18 years

The sanderling is about the size of a starling. It is one of the few shorebirds that can be identified by its feeding behaviour as it runs up and down a sandy beach just like a child following the waves in and out and trying not to get its feet wet. In winter plumage, it is pale grey above and white below and at any distance looks almost white. It has a short, straight, black beak and relatively short black legs. In flight it appears dark grey above with a thin, white wing stripe. It usually flies fast and straight, low over the water. In summer the head, breast and back become flecked and mottled rusty-brown. Usually silent on the ground, it sometimes gives a repeated, fairly high pitched *weeek* call in flight.

The sanderling can live for over eighteen years. Its common Irish name is *Luathrán*, which may refer to its habit of running quickly along the water's edge, while another Irish name *Laidhrín Geal* probably refers to its overall pale appearance. Another name

In flight with dunlin, a sanderling's paler colour is apparent.

that has been used to describe this bird in Ireland is the sea lark.

It breeds in patches of vegetation on Arctic tundra in Canada, Greenland, Svalbard (a group of islands located roughly halfway between Norway and the North Pole) and Siberia. Adults that have finished breeding arrive first in late August and early September followed by juveniles up to late September. It is thought that birds from Siberia remain here in the winter while birds from Greenland and Canada simply stop here to refuel before flying as far as South Africa to winter. The sanderling is site-faithful in winter and at migration staging sites. The spring migration to Siberia involves three long flights with two refuelling stops. It has the capability to fly 5,000 kilometres non-stop, quite an amazing feat for a bird that weighs only about 60 g/2 oz.

In winter the sanderling prefers non-estuarine, exposed, sandy beaches, but will sometimes be found in estuaries with firm, sandy areas and on stony or shingle beaches. It feeds on little worms and shrimp-like crustaceans which it snatches from the wet sand left by a breaking wave on the beach. It is rarely seen away from the coast. It can sometimes be seen searching for fly larvae in seaweed mounds along the shoreline. Up to 7,000 can be found in Ireland in the winter and highest concentrations have been recorded at Dublin Bay, Castlemaine Harbour and Rossbehy (Kerry) and Drumcliff Bay (Sligo).

Facing page:
A sanderling runs after a receding wave in search of prey in the wet sand.

Purple Sandpiper *Gobadán Cosbhuí*
Calidris maritima

Length	Wingspan	Weight	Oldest-known bird
20–22 cm	43–45 cm	65 g	20 years

The purple sandpiper would not be a familiar shorebird to most people in Ireland. At a distance it is a dull-looking bird. In winter plumage, its head is grey and upper breast, back and wings are mottled dark grey with white edges to some feathers. It is white below with grey flanks and grey spots and streaks on the breast and belly. The relatively long, slightly drooping beak, pale orange at the base and dark brown towards the tip and short yellow/orange legs are its most distinctive features. In summer plumage, it has purple-tinged feathers on the wings and back, from which it gets its name. It flies fast and direct and overall looks dark grey above, darkest on the rump and tail with a very thin, white wing stripe, paler below with white on the underwing and towards the undertail. It is not very vocal in the winter, often only making a high-pitched twittering call when disturbed.

The purple sandpiper can live for over twenty years. *Gobadán Cosbhuí* is its Irish name and very appropriately means 'yellow-legged sandpiper'. It breeds on Arctic tundra. It is thought that most purple sandpipers wintering in Ireland breed in Arctic Canada. It also winters farther north than most other waders, some staying well within the Arctic Circle all year round. Some populations are actually resident and do not migrate at all. To survive the extreme cold in more northerly latitudes, these birds have developed larger digestive systems than those wintering farther south, which allows them to eat more for their size and therefore generate more energy to keep them warm. Unlike most of our other waders, it lives almost exclusively on exposed rocky shores in winter. It feeds mainly on winkles, blue mussels, shrimps and other invertebrates, which it hunts on rocky shores and in seaweed on the tide line. It also feeds on all growth stages of the kelp fly where mounds of seaweed are found on the high-tide line.

The purple sandpiper is site-faithful during winter and returns to the same place in following winters. Up to 3,500 can be found in Ireland in winter. It has a very restricted distribution with highest concentrations by far having been recorded on the mid-Clare coast between Mal Bay and Doonbeg Bay with up to 400 birds, while a mere handful of other sites have recorded less than 100 birds each.

From top:
Map showing where the purple sandpiper can be found.

A flock of purple sandpipers (with one dunlin on the left) passing by.

A purple sandpiper stepping it out.

Dunlin *Breacóg*
Calidris alpina

Length	Wingspan	Weight	Oldest-known bird
16–22 cm	35–40 cm	48 g	28 years

The dunlin is a small wader, slightly bigger than a robin. In winter it is grey-brown above and white below with fine, dark streaking on the breast. Its black beak is long and slightly curved and its legs are black. Summer plumage is a complex pattern of browns, black and greys above and it develops a characteristic black belly patch. It flies very quickly when it shows a thin, white wing bar, a dark tail and a dark line running through its white rump. It is rarely seen alone and it feeds day and night where mud and sand are exposed, mainly on small invertebrates living close to the surface. Its call is a rather weak, grating *treee* usually heard in flight. Its song is a series of trills reminiscent, in a way, of the song of a hoarse robin.

The dunlin can live for over twenty-eight years. The common Irish name, *Breacóg*, refers to the speckling on its plumage. Another Irish name for it is *Cearc Ghainimh* which literally means 'Sand Hen'. Another name that has been used to describe this bird in Ireland is the sea lark. It breeds in Ireland in small numbers, probably fewer than 250 pairs, in sand-dune machair (low-lying coastal grassy plain), marshes and bogs in the northwestern half of the island. The number of breeding pairs in Ireland has declined over the last thirty years mainly owing to modern farming methods and afforestation. The dunlin also breeds all around the Arctic (circumpolar) in low Arctic and boreal habitats and winters in temperate and tropical areas, usually north of the equator. There is evidence to suggest that some Irish-born dunlin may spend the winter as far south as West Africa. The female departs the breeding grounds soon after the eggs hatch leaving the male to mind the young until they are old enough to fend for themselves. Juveniles leave the breeding grounds later than the adults, usually in September or October. In winter, it is one of our most numerous waders.

The dunlin has a mainly coastal distribution, preferring estuaries, mudflats and, to a lesser extent, sheltered bays, though it can also be found inland in small numbers. Anywhere there is mud on the coast, you are almost certain to see these small wanderers from almost every country in northern Europe. Flocks can range in size from fewer than 100 to over 10,000. Many dunlin also use Ireland as a stepping stone in spring and autumn on their journeys between their wintering grounds in northwest Africa and their

Facing page:
The dunlin, one of Ireland's most numerous shorebirds.

breeding grounds in northern Europe. The species has been well studied and as many as eleven different races have been identified, each with its own breeding ground, migration route and wintering ground. Three such races have been identified in Ireland. The *arctica* race breeds in northern Greenland and passes through on its way to and from its wintering grounds in West Africa. While *schinzii* does breed in Ireland and Britain, most of the race breeds in Iceland and southeast Greenland. Most winter in Mauretania and Senegal. Finally *alpina* breeds in Scandinavia and western Siberia. These comprise the majority of dunlin present here during the winter. Many of these stop to moult in the Wadden Sea (Netherlands) before arriving here for the winter. Studies have shown that they are highly site-faithful during and between winters. In mid-winter, up to half of the total west European population of dunlin are found in Ireland and Britain. In the winter the dunlin eats small molluscs, worms and crustaceans which it hunts by rapidly probing in mud or sand, sometimes in shallow water. Up to 138,000 are found here in winter and highest concentrations have been recorded at Shannon and Fergus Estuaries, Dundalk Bay (Louth) and Cork Harbour.

Facing page:
A dunlin resting on the shore exposed during low tide.

Below:
This dunlin stretches its long, pointed wing, typical of long-distance migrants.

Black-tailed Godwit *Guilbneach Earrdhubh*
Limosa limosa islandica

Length	Wingspan	Weight	Oldest-known bird
41–43 cm	75–77 cm	M: 280 g	23 years
		F: 340 g	

The black-tailed godwit is an elegant, long-legged and long-beaked wader of estuaries and wet grasslands. In winter plumage, when seen on the ground it looks overall grey above and pale below. Its beak is long, straight, pink at the base and dark towards the tip, the leg are long and dark. In summer plumage, the head, breast and belly turn rust-red but the undertail remains mainly white. In flight it looks completely different with a very noticeable broad, white wing stripe, a white rump and black band on the end of the tail, from which it gets its name. In flight it can be confused with an oystercatcher. Outside the breeding season it is usually not very loud but when close to a feeding flock some chattering sounds can usually be heard. As spring approaches it becomes noisier with more chattering and harsh calls often heard when it squabbles. It can sometimes be heard making a fast, high-pitched *wicka-wicka-wicka* call. Its loud, plaintive song can sometimes be heard just before it departs for Iceland to breed.

The black-tailed godwit can live for over twenty-two years. The Irish name, *Guilbneach Earrdhubh*, literally means 'black-tailed sharp beak'. Another name that has been used to describe this bird in Ireland is the red godwit. The black-tailed godwits that winter in Ireland breed in lowland wet grassland and marshes in Iceland. They are a distinct subspecies with a total world population of only about 60,000 individuals. There is only a handful of records of black-tailed godwits breeding in Ireland in the past. The most recent records are not more than two pairs breeding in any one year in the midlands and south between the late 1970s and mid-1980s.

In winter the Icelandic black-tailed godwits are found in Ireland and along the western seaboard of Europe and Morocco. Studies have shown that they prefer a habitat which includes mudflats and wet grasslands. It is not usually found on sandy beaches and avoids rocky shores. In the winter it feeds on marine invertebrates such as ragworms and small shellfish, usually on mudflats, and earthworms and insects on freshwater grasslands. When hunting it probes its long beak into the mud and can sometimes be seen repeatedly stabbing the mud in the same spot and pushing its beak so far down that it gets mud on its face.

Facing page:
A summer-plumaged black-tailed godwit in flight shows the black tail from which it gets its name.

109

Above:
A gust of wind unbalances black-tailed godwits roosting on one leg. They open their wings to maintain stability.

Facing page:
The head of a winter-plumaged black-tailed godwit almost completely submerged while probing mud in shallow water.

The black-tailed godwit is usually site-faithful both between and during winters. Studies have also shown that the male and female spend the winter in different parts of the godwits' wintering ground and reunite again on the breeding grounds the following summer. Largest numbers are found on our estuaries. Up to 18,000 are found in Ireland in winter representing about 30 per cent of the world population of this subspecies. Research shows that many more stop in Ireland before moving farther south and east. Highest concentrations have been recorded at Little Brosna Callows (Tipperary/Offaly border), Shannon and Fergus Estuaries, Cork Harbour, Dundalk Bay (Louth) and Ballymacoda (Cork).

Note: While the Icelandic subspecies has been increasing in population the European subspecies has declined in number by about 25 per cent in the last fifteen years, owing to the loss of nesting habitat resulting from agricultural intensification and wetland drainage, and is now classified as globally 'near threatened'.

Bar-tailed Godwit *Guilbneach Stríocearrach*
Limosa lapponica

Length	Wingspan	Weight	Oldest-known bird
38–39 cm	74–76 cm	M: 300 g F: 370 g	33 years

Unlike its close relative, the black-tailed godwit, the bar-tailed godwit prefers sandy beaches or firm mud where it hunts for one of its favourite prey: lugworms. In winter plumage, from above it looks grey with pale edges to most of the feathers. The tail is white with fine dark bars, from which it gets its name. In flight it has no obvious marking. It is pale below with fine streaking on the throat and breast. The long and slightly upturned beak is pink at the base and dark towards the tip. The legs are long and dark grey. In summer plumage, apart from the undertail, the underside becomes red-orange on the male, less so on the female. The feathers on the back are darker with pale red-brown spots. It is usually silent in the winter but sometimes makes a *kieruk kieruk* call in flight.

The bar-tailed godwit can live for over thirty-three years. The Irish name, *Guilbneach Stríocearrach,* means 'stripe-tailed sharp beak' referring to the barring on the tail, from which it gets its English name. Another name that has been used to describe this bird in Ireland is the godwin. The word 'godwit' is thought to come from old English and means 'good creature'. It is debatable as to whether this refers to it being a bird of good omen or that it was good to eat! The bar-tailed godwits found in Ireland breed on Arctic tundra in Scandinavia and northern Russia. Unlike its cousin the black-tailed godwit, it prefers sandier ground and so is found on the shore where this habitat occurs, which includes more exposed sandy beaches. Birds breeding in Scandinavia and western Russia tend to stay here for the winter, while birds from farther east seem to be passing through on their way to wintering grounds in West Africa. It is usually site-faithful during and between winters. In February and March most fly to the Wadden Sea (the Netherlands) where they put on fat for their migration to their Arctic breeding grounds. The bar-tailed godwit holds the world record for the longest non-stop flight. In 2007 a satellite-tagged bird flew 11,580 kilometres (7,200 miles) between Alaska and New Zealand in just nine days! In preparation for this astonishing flight it doubled its body mass and as much as 50 per cent of its body weight was pure fat, the fuel it would use to achieve this extraordinary feat.

As with the black-tailed godwit there is evidence that the males

Facing page:
Two bar-tailed godwits surrounded by knot take to the air.

winter in different geographical or habitat areas from the females. It hunts mainly small shellfish and a variety of marine worms but also shrimps and small marine snails by probing the ground with its long, straight beak. Up to 18,000 are found in Ireland in winter and highest concentrations have been recorded at Dundalk Bay (Louth), Dublin Bay and Wexford Harbour and Slobs.

Bar-tailed godwits roosting on a sandy beach.

Curlew *Crotach*
Numenius arquata

Length	Wingspan	Weight	Oldest-known bird
50–60 cm	80–100 cm	M: 770 g	31 years
		F: 1 kg	

The curlew is the largest European wader. The plumage of its upper parts is a complex pattern of browns and buffs. There is a conspicuous white triangle on the lower back and rump, and the tail is barred dark brown and white. Its underside is boldly streaked buff and black with white behind the legs. Its long and down-curving beak is distinctive, very dark brown with some pink at the base in young birds. Its long legs are dark blue-grey. The outer parts of the wings are darker brown than the rest of the wings and back, and apart from the white triangular patch on the lower back and rump it looks dark above. It can be seen flying singly or in loose flocks, lines or 'V's. The sounds of the curlew are synonymous with wild and remote places. It is one of the noisiest birds on a mudflat and its alarm call often sends every other bird within earshot into the air. Its call is a loud, lonely *cuur-lee*. It also makes softer *puurrring* noises. Its song is a series of bubbling trills.

The curlew can live for over thirty-one years. One of its Irish names is *Crotach* which means 'humped' and probably refers to its sometimes humpbacked appearance when hunting. Another Irish name is *Cúirliun* which may refer to its call, like its English name. Another name that has been used to describe this bird in Ireland is the Whaap. It is thought Whaap comes from a Scottish word 'Whaup' which means a mythical goblin with a long beak.

Unlike many of our wintering waders the curlew does not breed in Iceland. In Ireland, it breeds in areas of rough grazing and upland habitat mainly north of a line from Dundalk to Killarney. An estimated 12,000 were recorded breeding in Ireland during the Breeding Atlas Survey (1988–1991). Numbers have declined dramatically to just under 2,000 pairs in 2002 due mainly to land drainage and afforestation. This reflects an international decline, which is a serious worry for the future of this shorebird. Most curlews born in Ireland stay here for the winter and are joined by British-bred birds as well as many birds from northern Europe. It can be found anywhere on the island where mud is available under either salt or fresh water. It often feeds on earthworms in grassland. On mud it hunts mainly for worms, especially lugworms for which its beak is so well designed, but shellfish and even crabs will also be

eaten. Like other waders, if a curlew catches a crab it will usually shake it violently in its beak until the crab's legs fall off. It will then swallow the body whole and will often then pick up and swallow all the legs, leaving nothing to waste. It is site-faithful during and between winters and breeding seasons. Up to 66,000 are found here in winter and highest concentrations have been recorded at the Shannon and Fergus Estuaries, Cork Harbour and Lough Foyle.

Above:
The unmistakeable curlew, with its long, curved beak, takes to the air.

Facing page:
A curlew on salt marsh at high tide.

Above:
The olive-green legs, from which it gets its name are clearly visible on this greenshank.

Inset:
Unlike its close relative the redshank, the greenshank does not have white plumage on the wings

Greenshank *Laidhrín Glas*
Tringa nebularia

Length	Wingspan	Weight	Oldest-known bird
32 cm	69 cm	190 g	24 years

The greenshank is slightly smaller than a jackdaw. In winter its back is grey and its wings are grey towards the body and almost black towards the wing tips. The head, throat and breast are finely streaked grey and the belly and undertail are white. The slightly upturned grey beak is fairly long with a dark tip and the legs are olive-green. In breeding plumage, the back and wings are darker, with some obvious black spots and heavier marking on the neck and breast. In flight, a large, white triangle is visible on the lower back and rump, and the tail is white with faint grey barring. Unlike the redshank it has no white wing strips. Its most common call is a fairly rapid and explosive double *tieu-tieu* repeated a number of times, usually only heard when disturbed.

The greenshank can live for over twenty-four years. Its Irish name, *Laidhrín Glas,* refers to its green legs, just like its English name. One pair bred in Ireland at Achill in County Mayo in 1972 and 1974. This was the most westerly breeding site of its world breeding range. Apart from a few in Scotland, most breed in Scandinavia, northern Russia and Siberia in areas with lakes and marshland on taiga (cold, open, coniferous woodland) and forest areas. The female leaves shortly after the eggs hatch, leaving the male to feed the young until fledging. The male then leaves and is followed later by the young. Though it is not certain, it appears that many of the Scottish breeding population spend the winter in Ireland. Birds wintering in southern Europe and North Africa probably pass through Ireland each autumn. Compared to other waders, little is known of its movements.

The greenshank can be found on estuaries and coastal marshland but can also be found on freshwater shores inland. Unlike the redshank, the greenshank likes to hunt in pools and deeper water where it takes small crabs and shrimps and will often chase after small fish. It sometimes uses its feet to probe weed-covered areas in the hope of disturbing prey, which it then grabs. It is usually seen alone or in twos or threes, with some estuaries rarely recording more than 100 birds. Up to 1,700 are found here in winter and highest concentrations have been recorded at the Shannon and Fergus Estuaries, Strangford Lough (Down) and Lough Swilly.

Redshank *Cosdeargán*
Tringa totanus

Length	Wingspan	Weight	Oldest-known bird
27–29 cm	45–52 cm	M: 110 g F: 130 g	26 years

The redshank is a medium-sized wader slightly bigger than a blackbird. In winter on the ground it is grey-brown above, finely streaked on the throat and breast, paler on the belly and undertail. The bright orange-red legs are long. The orange-red beak is fairly short and straight with a dark tip. In summer plumage, it becomes browner above and more heavily streaked, spotted and barred underneath. The base of the beak and legs become brighter red. In flight a broad, white, trailing edge to the dark upper wing and a white triangle on the lower back and rump are characteristic.

The redshank is a very noisy bird when disturbed and utters a loud, harsh, repeated *tieuu-ieuu*. In the breeding season it makes a monotonous repeating *tiew-tiew-tiew* sound.

The redshank can live for over twenty-six years. Its Irish name, *Cosdeargán*, means 'little red leg' or 'little red-legged' and is identical to its English name in meaning. In Ireland it breeds in very small numbers on lowland and wet grassland mainly in the northern half of the island with the largest concentration in the west midlands and Connacht. Between 4,000 and 5,000 pairs were recorded breeding between 1988 and 1991 in the Breeding Atlas. It appears to be site-faithful from breeding season to breeding season and birds usually return to breed in the area where they were born. Irish-bred redshanks tend to stay in Ireland during the winter where they are joined by birds from the west of Iceland and northern Britain.

Facing page:
A redshank looks for prey at the water's edge.

Below left:
A redshank in flight; its white wing patches are not visible when on the ground.

A redshank wading in
shallow water.

Young birds tend to wander farther than adults in their first year or two. It appears to be very site-faithful during the winter. It is usually seen on estuaries in winter and feeds singly or in loose flocks, mainly on small worms and invertebrates found while probing in mud. When mud is freshly exposed on a falling tide a flock of redshanks will sometimes move across the mudflat spread out in a rough line and probe the mud for freshly exposed prey as they go. It has been shown to be particularly sensitive to cold weather when many die. It returns to its breeding grounds between March and April. Up to 32,600 can been found here in winter and highest concentrations are at Strangford Lough (Down), the Shannon and Fergus Estuaries and Cork Harbour.

Turnstone *Piardálaí Trá*
Arenaria interpres

Length	Wingspan	Weight	Oldest-known bird
22–23 cm	46 cm	120 g	21 years

The turnstone is slightly smaller than a blackbird. In winter it is dark grey-brown above with pale edges to the feathers giving a scaled effect. The head is paler grey-brown. The throat is white, and the breast dark brown with paler patches on the side of the breast, looking like a rounded 'W' pattern when seen head-on. The belly and undertail are white. The short, dark-brown bill is thick at the base and tapers to a fine tip and it has short, thick, bright orange legs. In April or May some will have moulted into summer plumage. Then the head, neck and breast form complex patterns of black and white, and orange-marmalade colours appear on the wings and back. The female is usually duller than the male. In flight the upper parts form a striking pattern of brown, black and white. It is rarely seen alone and sometimes can be found in flocks of up to 80 or 100 birds. Often reluctant to fly, it prefers to walk or run but if it does take to the air it flies fast and straight, usually low over the water. Call notes are variable but include a rapidly repeated *tuck-tuck-tuck,* often rising in pitch and speed towards the end. Lower piping notes are also heard. It can be heard calling on the ground, especially when fighting with each other and in flight.

The turnstone can live for over twenty-one years. Its Irish name is *Piardálaí Trá* which means 'beach rummager', an accurate name describing the way it searches for food by overturning rocks and seaweed. Another name that has been used to describe this bird in Ireland is the stone raw. Birds wintering in Ireland come from tundra breeding grounds in northeast Canada and northern Greenland. Shortly after the eggs hatch, the female leaves the male to look after the chicks until fledging, and it then leaves before the young. All have arrived here by the middle of September. It may fly directly here from Canada/Greenland or stop off in Iceland or even Norway. On passage in autumn, some birds from Scandinavia and Siberia stop off in Ireland on their way south to southern Europe and West Africa. It can be found almost anywhere along our coastline from late July to April, with a particular preference for rocky shorelines and stony beaches.

As its name suggests, it will often be heard turning stones in search of shrimps, sea snails and barnacles. It also looks for prey by turning seaweed where it is exposed at low tide or on the high-

Above:
A flock of turnstones heading away.

Facing page:
A turnstone on storm-driven
seaweed on the tide line.

tide line. Its diet is very varied and it can even be found eating fish scraps on piers. When it loses its bright summer plumage it becomes almost invisible on rocky or seaweed-covered shore. Also seen in estuaries where it will roost on buoys and boats, it is occasionally seen on inland lakes. Very small numbers are seen here in summer. It is very site-faithful during and between winters. Individuals form part of a flock of birds that will return to the same stretch of rocky shore, year after year, for their entire lives. Studies have shown that while the composition of wintering flocks largely remains constant they do not necessarily breed in the same place. Unlike many other waders, young birds do not wander any more than adults. It leaves for the breeding grounds usually in April and May. Early migrants tend to make the trip with one or a small number of stops, with most stopping off in Iceland on the way north, while late migrants probably fly non-stop from Ireland to northwest Greenland and northeast Canada. It is estimated that up to 14,000 turnstones spend the winter in Ireland each year. Highest concentrations have been recorded at Outer Ards (Down), Belfast Lough and the mid-Clare coast (Mal Bay to Doonbeg Bay).

Grey Heron (Crane) *Corr Éisc*
Ardea cinerea

Length	Wingspan	Weight	Oldest-known bird
90–96 cm	180–185 cm	1.5 kg	35 years

A familiar bird of the shore with its large dagger-shaped bill, white head, with a thick black stripe from the eye to the back of the head, long neck, grey body and long legs. In breeding plumage the adult has long, thin feathers on the neck and breast and two long, black feathers on the back of the head. The bill changes colour from dull yellow-orange to a bright pink. The grey heron in its first year has greyer plumage and a duller beak than the adult. Flight is ponderous on bowed wings with slow wingbeats, neck tucked up and legs trailing beyond its short tail. When it takes off or is disturbed it often gives a loud *frraank* call.

The grey heron can live for over thirty-five years. Its common Irish name, *Corr Éisc*, means 'fish beak'. It has a large selection of other Irish names including *Siubhán Fhada, Máire Fhada* or *Cáití Fhada* meaning 'long Siobhán' (or Mary or Kate). Other names used

Facing page:
A grey heron hunting in shallow water spots the movement of a fish on the surface.

Below:
A grey heron standing on a pier wall as a young herring gull looks on.

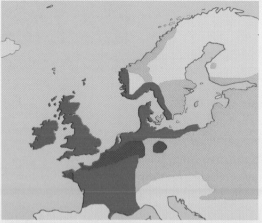

A grey heron in flight.

to describe this bird in Ireland include crane and Johnny-the-Bog.

The grey heron, which is Ireland's tallest bird, usually nests in colonies called heronries, which it frequents from January until late summer. About 3,650 pairs were found breeding in Ireland during the Breeding Atlas Survey (1988–1991). It is usually found in tall trees but, in the absence of trees, it will make its large nest on low bushes and even on the ground on isolated islands in the west. Some of the sounds of adults and young at the nest, heard at any time of day or night, are like a fairy-tale monster or someone getting sick!

The grey heron can be found almost anywhere there is suitable shallow water but less so on exposed coasts. It feeds mainly on fish, frogs, small animals and occasionally insects. Most are resident but are joined by some herons from northern Europe in the winter. Irish-born grey herons tend to stay here and not move very far from where they were born. It can often be seen silently stalking its prey at the water's edge, remaining motionless for ages then slowly moving its head closer to the water before striking at its prey with lightening speed. Sometimes it fishes on rivers or on the seashore in the middle of towns and cities and at night under artificial light. It never seems to get on with gulls and when flying over open water it will sometimes be chased relentlessly by them. As many as 10,000 are found in winter in Ireland and highest concentrations have been recorded at Lough Neagh and Galway Bay.

Little Egret *Éigrit Bheag*
Egretta garzetta

Length	Wingspan	Weight	Oldest-known bird
60–65 cm	90–95 cm	450 g	22 years

Smaller and slimmer than the much larger grey heron, the little egret is the only all-white heron seen on the shore. It has snow-white plumage, a long, dark, dagger-shaped beak and black legs with yellow feet. In breeding plumage, it develops long, thin, white feathers from the back of the head and lace-like feathers on the back. In flight the little egret flies slowly with bowed wings with neck tucked up and yellow feet visible on legs trailing beyond its short tail. It is usually silent but will make squawking noises when fighting or at the nest.

The little egret can live to be over twenty-two years old. As a new regular visitor to our shores, its Irish name, *Éigrit Bheag*, like the English name, comes from the French word *Aigrette*, which means 'little heron'. Up to the 1980s this bird was rarely seen in Ireland. Since then, numbers have increased dramatically and in

A little egret runs across the mud in an aggressive display, leaving drops of water mid-air in its wake.

The little egret, unmistakeable in flight with its snow-white plumage and yellow feet.

This map is only a rough guide to wintering areas. No national data is currently available for breeding areas.

Above:
The little egret, unmistakeable in flight with its snow-white plumage and yellow feet.

Facing page:
A little egret watches for the movement of a small fish or shrimp in shallow water. Little egret were once hunted for their plummage used to adorn hats

1997 the first record of breeding in Ireland was made. Now it breeds in a number of counties, mainly in the south and east. Nests are usually found in a heronry (where the much larger grey heron breeds). When hunting, it seems to prefer estuaries and sheltered bays.

It has a broad diet and in Ireland feeds mainly on small fish, shrimps, and invertebrates. Unlike its taller cousin, the grey heron, the little egret is a much more active hunter and will often be seen running after its prey, sometimes with wings flicking open now and then. It has a curious habit of shuffling one of its feet in shallow water and running after and stabbing at anything edible that is disturbed. At high tide, groups roost in trees not too far from their feeding area. In winter these roosts can be easy to see as their white plumage stands out against the trees. Highest concentrations are on the south and east coast with as many as 300 pairs now breeding in Ireland.

Facing page, top:
Some shorebirds do not breed or winter in Ireland and are only seen passing through on migration. The curlew sandpiper, with its relatively long beak, is one such bird.

Facing page, bottom:
The common sandpiper breeds inland but can be seen on the seashore during migration in spring and autumn on their way to and from Africa, and rarely during winter.

Above:
The snipe is usually associated with bogs and marshes but will sometime move to estuaries in winter. Their 'cryptic' plumage allows them to become almost invisible in the vegetation just above the tide line.

Left:
The ruff, which gets its name from the male's elaborate head and neck breeding plumage, is seen in small numbers on our shores mainly during its autumn migration.

133

Ducks, Geese and Swans

There are 158 species worldwide and 48 species have been
recorded in Ireland.

A flock of brent geese flying
between feeding areas.

Brent Goose *Gé Dhubh*
Branta bernicula

Length	Wingspan	Weight	Oldest-known bird
58–62 cm	115–125 cm	1.5 kg	28 years

The brent goose has a black head, neck and breast with white 'gill' marks on the side of the neck. The upper parts are dark grey-brown and the tail is white with a narrow black edge. The belly is light grey-brown while the area under the tail is white. The legs and short bill are black. In their first winter young birds travel and stay close to the parents. These young birds look similar to adults but usually lack the white neck marks and have white edges to some of the wing feathers. This difference in plumage allows researchers to identify family groups and they can learn how successful their breeding season has been by comparing the family sizes from year to year. In flight the brent goose looks dark except for the white on the tail and undertail which is very noticeable. It flies with fast wingbeats and usually does not fly in classic V-formation, the flock shape ranging from long loose lines to bunched groups, often flying low over water. Often the first suggestion of the presence of brent geese is their muted, quivering *grough* sound. They are often silent on their own.

The brent goose can live for over twenty-eight years. In Irish it is called the *Gé Cadhan*. It is uncertain what *Cadhan* refers to. Another Irish name for the brent goose is *Gé Dhubh* which means 'the black goose'. This is a very appropriate name because if you come across a flock on the shore they can be hard to see since they blend very well with the dark-coloured rocks and seaweed. The brent goose is the smallest and most marine of our wintering geese. The species comprises three distinct subspecies which breed and winter in different parts of the northern hemisphere and those visiting Ireland are almost all of the pale-bellied subspecies (*hrota*), which breeds on lowland tundra plains in Arctic Canada, mainly on Queen Elizabeth Island and Bathurst Island in northern Canada, while, for example, in southeast Britain the subspecies tends to be the dark-bellied subspecies (*bernicla*), which nests mainly in central Arctic Russia. It seems to prefer breeding near gull colonies or a bird of prey as it is thought it helps protect them from predation by ground hunters such as foxes.

Because the brent goose mostly eats vegetable matter, and therefore has to eat a lot to keep up energy supplies, almost all our brent geese take a two-to-three-week refuelling stop on the west coast of Iceland while going to and coming from their breeding grounds. Most start leaving the breeding grounds in late August with most here

Facing page:
Brent geese catching the slipstream of the bird in front.

in Ireland by the end of October. The total distance between breeding grounds and wintering grounds here is over 4,500 kilometres and some fly over 1,600 kilometres non-stop. Up to 80 per cent of the world's light-bellied brent geese stop off in Strangford Lough in County Down before most spread out to spend the winter on other Irish estuaries. Unlike other geese it is found regularly on estuaries and on any coastal habitat where its food is found in inter-tidal areas. It favours eel grass or seagrass (*zostera*) and can often be seen upending like a mallard to reach its food when covered by the tide. Its winter distribution has been closely linked to this marine plant which grows usually on sandy ground of intertidal areas. In recent years it has been seen feeding on grass in increasing numbers on pasture and stubble fields, golf courses, playing fields and park grasslands. The brent goose has been well studied in Ireland and it has been shown to remain in family groups throughout the winter, like other geese. It has also been discovered that food availability mainly determines its movements around the island. It is possible to find it singly or in small numbers away from its regular locations in suitable habitats anywhere in Ireland.

Brent geese start heading for the breeding grounds in late March and early April. The total midwinter population in Ireland is about 20,000 but this is highly variable from year to year, depending on breeding success. The largest winter concentrations have been recorded in Strangford Lough (Down), Dublin Bay and Lough Foyle.

Below from left:
A brent goose searching in the shallows for its favourite food, eel grass.

The white-edged wing feathers of a brent goose born this year contrast with the dark wing feather of the adult feather of its parent behind.

Shelduck *Lacha Bhreac*
Tadorna tadorna

Length	Wingspan	Weight	Oldest-known bird
58–71 cm	110–133 cm	M: 1.2 kg F: 1.0 kg	24 years

The shelduck is Ireland's largest duck and is rarely seen inland. In appearance it is unmistakeable with a mainly white body, chestnut breast band, a thick black line down the centre of the belly, a dark-green head which looks black in dull light conditions, red bill and pink legs. Females are smaller than males, lack the red knob at the base of the beak and have almost no black on the belly. Newly fledged young are similar in shape to the adults but are mainly black and white, lacking the bright colours of the adults. When it takes to the air black 'braces' on the back and black on the wings can be seen. It is usually vocal only during the breeding season. Loud calls include a rapid guttural, laughing *agh-agh-agh-agh*, lasting several seconds. It also gives a very high liquid *tiew-tiew* with a very high whistle.

The shelduck can live for over twenty-four years. In Irish it is called the *Lacha Bhreac* which means 'the pied duck' or *Lacha Chriosrua* which means 'red-belted duck' referring to the chestnut band on its breast. Other names used to describe this bird in Ireland include sheldrake and bar duck. About 4,650 pairs were found breeding in Ireland during the Breeding Atlas Survey (1988–1991) mainly along the east and south coasts. Shelduck nest in holes and cavities of all types, from rabbit burrows to discarded large plastic drums. Clutches can contain up to eleven young.

Like all ducks the young leave the nest almost immediately and

A shelduck preening.

are led to water by the parents. This can be a perilous journey for the young, especially if the nest is far from the shore, because they are very vulnerable to attack by predators such as foxes, hooded crows and grey herons. Once they reach the relative safety of the water they are often protected in a crèche containing two to four broods guarded by one or two adults. After breeding almost all our adult shelduck migrate to Heligoland Bight in the Wadden Sea off the Dutch/German/Danish coast to moult, probably in one non-stop flight, returning to Irish estuaries from September onwards, possibly with a number of stops along the way. The shelduck in its first year generally does not migrate to Heligoland. Some birds from Germany, the Netherlands and Belgium come here for the winter. The shelduck prefers estuaries and sheltered coasts where it searches for small snails and worms on or near the surface of soft mud by swinging its beak from side to side in a scythe-like fashion and sifting out the food with its beak and tongue. Up to 15,000 are found in Ireland in winter and highest concentrations have been recorded in Strangford Lough (Down), Cork Harbour, the Shannon and Fergus Estuaries and Dublin Bay.

Facing page:
A female shelduck at rest.

Above:
Two male shelduck in chase. They can be identified by the large knob at the base of the beak.

141

Wigeon *Lacha Rua*
Anas penelope

Length	Wingspan	Weight	Oldest-known bird
45–51 cm	75–86 cm	M: 800 g	34 years
		F: 650 g	

The wigeon is smaller than the mallard. The male has a dark red-brown head with a conspicuous creamy forehead and crown. Its body is mainly grey with a grey-pink breast, grey flanks, a white belly and a white patch at the rear of the flanks. The area under the tail is black. It has a short, blue-grey bill with a black tip. As with most ducks the female is duller but identical to the male in shape, grey-brown with a pale belly. During moult the male plumage resembles that of the female. When it takes to the air it rises quickly from water or land. In flight white wing patches on the inner part of the wing of the male only can be clearly seen, and both male and female have dark-green patches on the trailing edge of the wing. The male utters a distinctive,

Facing page:
A male wigeon or *Lacha Cheann-rua* (red-headed duck).

Below:
In flight the white wing patches of the male wigeon can be clearly seen.

high-pitched, whistling *feeoow*, which can be heard at some distance while the female makes a lower guttural sound.

The wigeon can live to be over thirty-four years old. The Irish names, such as *Lacha Cheann-rua*, meaning 'red-headed duck' refer to the male's distinctive reddish head. Other names used to describe this bird in Ireland include golden head and yellow poll. There is a small breeding population, fewer than twenty-five pairs, primarily along the River Shannon. Most of our wigeon come to spend the winter in Ireland from breeding grounds in Iceland, northern Europe and northern Russia, arriving in the autumn and departing abruptly in March. It is known to be site-faithful during the

winter, often returning to the same area year after year. It is a surface-feeding duck mainly seen on the coast, usually in estuaries, where it feeds on grasses and algae but can be found inland also. Tight flocks can sometimes be seen grazing on grass in fields, usually not far from water. If disturbed while grazing, they will usually fly back to the water, swimming ashore and walking back to the grass once danger has passed. Rarely encountered on its own, this duck can be seen in flocks of over 1,000 birds. Very cold snaps can lead to an influx of more wigeon to Ireland from continental Europe. One thing that might help you to remember how to identify a male wigeon is to think of pigeon, because the woodpigeon has similar colours. Up to 90,000 wigeon are found in Ireland in winter and highest concentrations have been recorded in Lough Foyle, Little Brosna Callows (Tipperary/Offaly border) and Castlemaine Harbour (Kerry).

A male and female wigeon feeding in shallow water.

Teal *Praslacha*
Anas crecco

Length	Wingspan	Weight	Oldest-known bird
34–38 cm	58–64 cm	330 g	21 years

The teal is one of our smallest surface-feeding ducks. The male has a chestnut head and neck, dark-green eye-patches extending down the side of the neck, a horizontal white line above the closed wing and a pale-yellow undertail outlined in black. The female looks all grey-brown. During moult the male plumage resembles that of the female. When taking to the air it rises quickly on rapid wingbeats. In flight it looks fairly plain. On males and females green and white patches can be seen on the trailing edge of the wing in good light and at close range. In winter, flocks of these birds can be very noisy. The male makes a short, low, bell-sounding *krreet*, while the female makes a much higher quack.

The teal can live for over twenty-one years. A few of its Irish names, such as *Praslacha*, refer to it being a fast flying duck. Once a relatively common breeding bird, it has declined significantly. About 675 pairs were found breeding in Ireland during the Breeding Atlas Survey (1988–1991) and those appear to stay here all year round. It usually breeds on a variety of inland lakes and ponds. Males play no part in rearing the young. It is widespread and common in the winter, not just on the coast where it prefers estuaries, but also inland. Because it mainly needs wet mud to feed, during very cold snaps it will often move long distances in search of ice-free feeding areas. On such rare icy occasions in Ireland, birds seem to move south to France, Spain and Portugal. In the winter Irish birds are joined by teal from Iceland, Scandinavia and as far as northwest Siberia. Most of the Icelandic population (fewer than 1,000) winter in Ireland.

Teal eat a wide variety of food from seeds to small invertebrates. They return to breeding grounds any time between late February and May. Weather conditions seem to determine where they breed and they tend not to be site-faithful. Unlike many other shorebirds, the teal could be described as a nomad with no fixed abode that will move either its breeding or wintering grounds in response to local weather conditions. Up to 57,000 are found in Ireland in winter and highest concentrations have been recorded in the Shannon and Fergus Estuaries, Little Brosna Callows (Tipperary/Offaly border) and Lough Ree.

Facing page:
Three female and one male teal sift for small snails in the soft mud.

Teal are very fast fliers.

Pintail *Biorearrach*
Anas acuta

Length	Wingspan	Weight	Oldest-known bird
57–59 cm	87–89 cm	M: 900 g F: 700 g	27 years

The pintail, a very elegant looking bird, is slightly larger than the mallard. The male has a chocolate-brown head with a thin, white line running up the side of its relatively long, thin neck. Its body is mainly grey with a white breast, grey flanks, a white belly and a buff patch at the rear of the flanks. The back has long, thin, black feathers with buff edges. The area under the long, pointed tail, from which it gets its English name, is black. It has a short, blue-grey bill with a black tip. As with most ducks the female is duller, though noticeably paler than a female mallard. Identical in shape to the male, it lacks the long, pointed tail. During moult the male plumage resembles that of the female. When it takes to the air it rises quickly from water or land. In flight, both male and female have dark-green patches with a white trailing edge on the wing. Usually quiet, the sounds are not unlike those of the mallard. The male makes a squeaking *whee-hee* call, rising in pitch in the middle and the female makes low, quacking sounds.

Facing page:
Pintail-the name is self explanatory.

Below:
A male and female pintail in flight.

149

More brightly-coloured male pintails accompanied by brown-plumaged females.

The pintail can live to be over twenty-seven years old. The Irish names *Biorearrach* meaning 'spike tail' and *Lacha Stiúrach* meaning 'rudder duck' refer to its long tail.

It is one of our rarest breeding ducks and only nine pairs were found breeding in Ireland between 1998 and 2002, mainly in the northeast. Most of our pintail come here to spend the winter, migrating from breeding grounds in Iceland, northern Europe and northern Russia. Males leave the breeding grounds to moult once the females start incubating the eggs. Almost all have arrived here by the end of October. There is evidence that some pintails pass through Ireland on the way south to southern Europe and even North Africa. Very cold snaps can lead to an influx of more pintail to Ireland from continental Europe. Most have left for their breeding grounds by the

beginning of April. They are unusual among ducks in that they are mainly found concentrated in just a few locations and this is reflected in their distribution in Ireland. They eat mainly small snails and also seeds. Up to 2,000 pintail are found in Ireland in winter mostly at the coast, with highest concentrations having been recorded at Tacumshin Lake (Wexford), Strangford Lough (Down) and Dublin Bay.

A close view of a female pintail.

Mute swans often spend the winter on our seashore, eating seaweeds and begging for food from anyone they come across.

The mallard would be familiar to anyone visiting their local pond or park but many spend the winter on our estuaries.

Gulls and Terns

There are over fifty gull species worldwide and twenty-one species recorded in Ireland. There are forty-four species of tern worldwide and fourteen species recorded in Ireland.

A little tern rides the sea breeze along the Wicklow coast.

Black-headed Gull *Faoileán an Chaipín*
Larus ridibundus

Length	Wingspan	Weight	Oldest-known bird
35–40 cm	94–105 cm	M: 330 g F: 250 g	30 years

The black-headed gull is slightly smaller than a rook. The adult in winter has pale grey on the wings and back, with a white leading edge and black tips to the outer wing feathers. The head is white with a dark spot behind the eye. The rest of the body is white. The short, straight beak is red with a black tip and the legs are red. In summer it looks the same except its head is chocolate-brown, not black, and the beak and legs become deep red. Immature birds have brown on the wings and a dark band on the end of the tail. The legs are orange-yellow and the beak is pale brown-yellow with a black tip. They are identical in size and shape to the adults. In flight the adult is pale grey on the back and wings. There is a white leading edge to the outer part of the very pointed wing forming a long, thin, white triangle, visible from above and below, with a black trailing edge. Immature birds have brown on the wings and a dark trailing edge to the inner part of the wing also. There is a dark band on the end of the tail. It sometimes circles and soars in loose small flocks on warm thermals in vulture-like fashion. It can be very noisy, especially when feeding. Calls are higher in pitch than the larger gulls, and include a thin-sounding drawn-out *kaaww*, and also a softer chatter, especially when not excited or when washing.

The black-headed gull can live for over thirty years. It has a number of Irish names, some of uncertain origin. One is *Faoileán an Chaipín* which means 'the gull with the little cap' while *Faoileán Ceanndubh* literally means 'black headed gull'. Other names used to

Facing page:
In winter the black-headed gull replaces its dark hood with white plumage and a dark smudge behind the eye.

Left:
In summer plumage the gull is not 'black-headed' but, in fact, chocolate-headed. The gaps in the wings indicate that this bird is moulting.

159

describe this bird in Ireland include redshank gull, red-legged gull, pine and pine maw.

It might be surprising to learn that, unlike most other seagulls, the black-headed gull breeds away from the coast, mainly in the midlands, west and north of the country on bogs, marshes, brackish lagoons and islands. An estimated 14,000 pairs were found breeding in Ireland between 1998 and 2002. It is suggested that it has declined by as much as 70 per cent since the 1980s as a breeding species. Most Irish-bred birds remain in Ireland though some will migrate south to France, Spain and Portugal in the winter. From July onwards, young birds, with their noticeable brown marking on the back of the neck and side of the breast, and adults begin to appear away from the breeding colonies, especially in estuaries. It is more common on the east and south coasts. By mid-winter it is our most numerous gull species and is found all over the country. The most migratory of our gulls, large numbers of black-headed gulls come here each winter from Britain, Scandinavia, continental Europe, Iceland and even Russia.

The black-headed gull's diet is very broad, ranging from spiders and flying ants to fish, worms and carrion. It is rarely seen on its own and is at home feeding on a mudflat, rocky shore, playing field or refuse tips, behind fishing boats or tractors. It appears to be site-faithful during and between winters. Night roosts containing many thousands of birds can be found on water in large bays and estuaries around the coast. These birds start heading back to their breeding grounds from February onward. Black-headed gulls are hunted in Scandinavia and the Iberian Peninsula. Up to 45,000 are found in Ireland in winter and highest concentrations have been recorded at Dundalk Bay (Louth), Belfast Lough and Outer Ards (Down).

A black-headed gull drops its wings and arches its neck in a threat display. This pose is also used during courtship.

Herring Gull *Faoileán Scadán*
Larus argentatus

Length	Wingspan	Weight	Oldest-known bird
55–67 cm	130–158 cm	M: 1.2 kg F: 948 g	34 years

The herring gull is as big as a mallard. The adult has a white body, light-grey back and wings, and black-and-white wing tips. The legs are pink, the short, stout beak is yellow with a red spot and the iris is yellow. In winter, the head and neck can become mottled grey-brown. Immature birds have a dirty grey-brown head and body and the upper part of the wings are a complex pattern of brown, black and buff. The wing tips are dark brown. The beak is black, the iris is usually dark and there is a black band on the end of the tail. The plumage changes gradually to reach adult plumage over four years. In flight the adult has a light blue-grey back and wings above with black-and-white wing tips (much more black than white). There is a thin, white trailing edge to the wings. Immature birds have varying amounts of brown on the body and wings, usually with no white

A young herring gull showing the typical brown plumage not seen on adults.

at the wing tips. In strong winds it will glide on bowed wings high over land and sea. Calls include a loud repeated *kuwaa* and a laugh-like *agah-ga-ga*.

The herring gull can live for over thirty-four years. Its Irish name, *Faoileán Scadán*, means 'herring gull' just like the English name. Other names used to describe this bird in Ireland include silver-back, silvery gull and laughing gull. This large gull is found not only all along our coast but also inland, especially in winter. It makes its nest, usually in long grass or under tall weeds, at the top of sea cliffs or on offshore islands. In recent years it has taken to nesting on rooftops, mainly in Dublin, which to the herring gull, are cliffs and islands. An estimated 6,500 pairs were found breeding in Ireland between 1998 and 2002. The herring gull is very noisy and will defend its territory during the breeding season with great energy. It will dive at anything that intrudes, sometimes even hitting the intruder with its bill or wings. Irish herring gulls do not usually travel very far, sometimes to Britain but only rarely leaving the country. In winter Irish herring gulls are joined by birds from Britain. It is a scavenger with a broad diet and so will be found anywhere there is a possibility of a free meal, such as at rubbish dumps, around fishing boats or along the shoreline, especially around outflow pipes. Up to 12,000 individuals have been found here in winter and highest concentrations have been recorded at Belfast Lough and Rogerstown Estuary (Dublin).

Facing page and this: Adult herring gulls in flight.

Little Tern *Geabhróg Bheag*
Sternula albifrons

Length	Wingspan	Weight	Oldest-known bird
22 cm	52 cm	56 g	23 years

Noticeably smaller than our other terns, the little tern is a summer visitor to our shores. It has a short, deeply forked white tail. The back and wings are light grey with a dark leading edge to the outer part of the wing. The rest of the body is white with a black cap with a distinctive white forehead. The white on the forehead becomes more extensive in the autumn and winter. Unlike our other terns the adult has a bright-yellow beak with a dark tip and the short legs are yellow-orange. The beak becomes darker after breeding. Young birds have black V-shaped marks on the wings and the wing tips are darker than the adult. The white on the forehead is more extensive and not as neat-looking as the adult. In flight the short, forked tail, long wings, quick wingbeats and its downward pointing head when hunting are notable features. It often hovers before diving. The call usually is a loud high-pitched *wick-wick*.

The little tern can live for over twenty-three years. Its Irish name, *Geabhróg Bheag*, means 'Little Chatterer'. This, the smallest of the Irish terns, is usually the first to reach our shores in April from its wintering grounds in West Africa, and the last to leave in September. Continuing its habit of being different to our other tern species, the little tern rarely nests far from the seashore. Because of its preference for sandy and shingle beaches it is mainly found nesting on the east coast south of Dundalk and on the west coast north of Tralee Bay. About 206 pairs were found breeding in Ireland during the All-Ireland Tern Survey in 1995 and the largest colonies are found in counties Wicklow,

Our smallest tern and the only one with a yellow beak with a black tip.

Wexford, Kerry and Mayo. Because the little tern likes to nest close to the shore it has come under increasing pressure from human activities such as beach walking, and the number of breeding pairs has dropped from 315 in 1969–'70. Its nest is usually just a depression in the sand or stones and so can be easily washed away by the sea during a storm or spring tides, and is vulnerable to predators such as foxes and rats as well as domestic dogs. Little terns are not very faithful to breeding sites and will sometimes move from year to year, making it difficult to protect their vulnerable nesting colonies which, unlike other terns, rarely exceed forty nests in number.

The little tern rarely travels far from the shore when hunting. Like all terns, the little tern feeds by plunging from the air, hovering frantically before dropping straight into the sea with a splash, hunting small fish such as sand eels and sprat and shrimps.

A little tern in flight.

Common Tern *Geabhróg*
Sterna hirundo

Length	Wingspan	Weight	Oldest-known bird
31–35 cm	82–95 cm	130 g	33 years

The common tern is smaller than the sandwich tern. The adult has a black crown and forehead in the summer with the forehead turning white in the winter. Its body and forked tail are white. The upper wings and back are pale grey and the wing tips dark grey-black. The short, thin beak is red with a black tip and the legs are short and red. Young birds have a white forehead and dark-edged feathers giving a scaled effect to the back and wings, darkest on the leading edge of the inner part of the wing. In flight it looks very buoyant on the wing; it has strong, deep wingbeats and often glides and circles before diving. It is very noisy at the breeding colony. Calls include a drawn-out, descending *keeeeeey*, and high, rapid *kirree-kirree-kirree*.

The common tern can live for over thirty-three years. Its common Irish name is *Geabhróg* which means 'chatterer' and another, *Scréachóg*

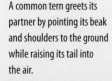

A common tern greets its partner by pointing its beak and shoulders to the ground while raising its tail into the air.

Thrá, means 'beach screecher' both referring to its loud, raucous calls. Other names used to describe this bird in Ireland include pirre (from Northern Ireland, apparently because of one of its calls) and kingfisher. Sailors called it the sea-swallow because of its long, forked tail. It usually arrives here in late April or early May and departs for its wintering grounds on the West African coast in September. It breeds in colonies around our coast, mainly in the northern half of the country and on inland lakes, such as on the Shannon, Lough Erne and Lough Neagh. About 4,189 pairs were found breeding in Ireland during the All-Ireland Tern Survey in 1995. Numbers have been declining here in recent years and there is a noticeable northward shift in their breeding range. It is suggested that global warming may be the cause. It is our most widely distributed breeding tern and will sometimes nest on man-made structures such as barges, rafts and undisturbed docklands. It will defend its nest, dive at any intruder, sometimes striking it with is needle-sharp beak. It feeds mainly on sand eels and sprats which it catches by plunging head-first into the water and flying off immediately.

Like all terns, the common tern rarely lands on water, preferring beaches, rocky shores, small islands, moored boats and buoys. As many as 11,000 terns, mostly common terns, roost at low tide on the vast expanse of the beach on the south side of Dublin Bay in late summer and autumn. A common tern ringed on Copeland Island, County Down, in May 1959 was found in Victoria, Australia, in October 1968, over 17,000 kilometres away.

167

Facing page:
A common tern banks before diving to catch a sprat near the surface of the sea

Above:
An adult glaucous gull on the left and a young Iceland gull in the background on the right, often referred to as 'northern gulls' because they breed in Iceland and Greenland and come to our shores each winter in small numbers. They stand out from our own gulls because they never have dark wing tips.

Left:
An adult Mediterranean gull can resemble a black-headed gull but has no black on the wings

Above: The common gull usually nests on inland lakes but is often seen on the shore in winter.
Below: Like most gulls the great black-backed gull will often patrol the shore for food.

Above:
The lesser black-backed gull is so called because the colour of the adults' back (and wings) is not as black as its larger relative, the great black-backed gull.

Right:
The sandwich tern is our largest tern and the adult has an all-black beak with a yellow tip.

Honorary Shorebirds

Birds such as waders, ducks and gulls are readily associated with the shore but a wide variety of birds normally classified as land birds also hunt on the shore to a greater or lesser extent. The rock pipit is a true shorebird, rarely venturing far from the shore, nesting nearby and hunting in the intertidal area. While hooded crows are found all over Ireland, those on the coast regularly hunt on the shore, especially in the winter. Other opportunistic land birds such as starlings, wagtails and finches will sometimes search for food on seaweed on the high-tide line and almost any land bird may occasionally turn up on the shore.

A northern wheatear stops to 'refuel' by fattening up on insects found on seaweed on the shore before continuing its migration south to Africa.

Rock Pipit *Riabhóg Chladaigh*
Anthus petrosus

Length	Wingspan	Weight	Oldest-known bird
17 cm	24 cm	24 g	11 years

Slightly bigger than a robin, the rock pipit like a duller, smoky version of its close relative the meadow pipit. Its back and wings are dark grey or olive-brown with indistinct dark streaking on the back. Light-grey underparts are heavily streaked. The outer tail feathers are pale grey, not white. The short, thin beak is all dark in the summer and pale yellow at the base in winter and the long, thin legs are dark brown. In flight the pale grey outer tail feathers are not always very noticeable and its flight pattern is undulating and looks dull and featureless with a long tail. The outer tail feathers are pale grey and not always very noticeable. Its call is a thin, repeated *tweep*. During the breeding season its song is a series of high-pitched notes increasing in speed and decreasing in pitch before ending in a fast trill. Like its close relative the meadow pipit, it has a song flight where it flies up into the air, singing, and descends slowly, parachute-like, on half-closed wings.

Facing page:
The rock pipit's dull plumage allows it to blend in with its seashore habitat.

Below:
A rock pipit hunting insects from a branch on a piece of driftwood to feed a hungry brood of chicks.

The rock pipit can live for over ten years. Its Irish name, *Riabhóg Chladaigh*, roughly means 'little, streaked thing of the shore'. In the west it is also known as *Circín Trágha* which means 'beach chick'. Its name clearly indicates its favoured habitat – rocky seashores – and it is rarely seen away from the coast. Found almost all around Ireland, the only gaps are where sand replaces rock and gravel shoreline especially on the east coast south of Strangford Lough in County Down. It nests among rocks usually close to the high-tide line and will raise two broods each year. The cuckoo sometimes lays its eggs in the nests of rock pipits. The rock pipit rarely travels far and will defend its territory all year round. It feeds on a wide variety of invertebrates including flies, midges and their larvae but also shellfish, small fish and even plant seeds which it finds under rocks and seaweed above or below the high tide mark.

About 12,500 pairs were found breeding in Ireland during the Breeding Atlas Survey (1988–1991), with highest numbers on the west coast.

Hooded Crow *Feannóg*
Corvus cornix

Length	Wingspan	Weight	Oldest-known bird
47 cm	97–99 cm	510 g	Over 17 years

Some hooded crows spend a lot of time hunting on the seashore. Bigger than a rook, it has a black hood that covers the head, neck and breast and forms a rough-edged bib. On young birds the hood is not well defined and can look dark brown around the edges. The rest of the body is pale grey-brown. The wings and tail are black, the black beak is stout and the legs are dark. In flight, unlike the other crows it has an obvious pale, grey-brown back and when moulting the wings can sometimes look striped black and white. Its call is usually a loud hoarse *krraaa-krraaa-krraaa*, often made while bobbing its head up and down.

The hooded crow can live for over seventeen years. Its common Irish name, *Feannóg*, may come from the word *Fionnóg* which means 'someone who skins animals'. This would relate to its habit of eating carrion away from the shore or from the word *fean* which means 'a fan', a possible reference to the fact that it often fans its tail when calling. Other names used to describe this bird in Ireland include grey crow, scald crow, hoodie, blue-backed crow, hen crow and bunting crow. This is the most widespread of the crow family, though not as abundant as the rook. Unlike the rook it does not nest in colonies, preferring to nest in single pairs, usually in trees, but where none are available it will use cliff ledges, shrubs and even the ground itself. In Britain, the hooded crow is confined to Scotland and the Isle of Man, and is replaced elsewhere by its close relative the carrion crow, which has all-black plumage. It has a wide taste in food, including insects, amphibians, small birds, grain and carrion, which partly explains why it is so widespread. It is the only crow that regularly gathers food on the seashore, where it can often be seen flying up from the shore and dropping shellfish onto the rocks or the road to break them open, resulting in large numbers of broken shells left mysteriously on top of walls and on coastal roads. About 290,000 pairs were found breeding in Ireland during the Breeding Atlas Survey (1988–1991).

Facing page:
A signpost rusty from sea salt provides this hooded crow with an ideal vantage point.

Right:
This combined sequence of images shows a hooded crow flying up and dropping a large clam onto the rock.

Facing page:
Most people are surprised when they see a kingfisher on a pier or large rock on the seashore in winter but many 'migrate' from their breeding areas on our rivers.

Clockwise from top:
Pied wagtails that live near the coast will often search for insects on seaweed piled up on a beach or strand after a storm o spring tide.

Starlings that live near the shore will often search for insects and grubs amongs seaweed on the high-tide line.

Rooks, more usually seen on open farmland, will sometimes hunt for worm on muddy shores.

The Future for our Shorebirds

Global warming will probably be the biggest challenge for our shorebirds. As has been shown in this book, they travel vast distances and, for their survival, depend on habitats as diverse as high-Arctic tundra and tropical and subtropical wetlands. If any creatures on the planet are going to feel the effects of global warming, shorebirds will. Birds time their breeding season to coincide with a peak in food supply for their young. On the breeding grounds climate change is already having an effect with the timing of breeding and the peak in food supply beginning to separate at a rate too fast for shorebirds to adapt. This will lead to birds hatching young with less food present to feed them than before. At least 38 per cent of arctic-nesting shorebirds are decreasing in number and population trends are unknown for 25 per cent. More than 50 per cent of shorebirds in the Eurasia–East Africa Flyway are declining in numbers. Permafrost in the Arctic is melting, causing the habitat to change and become unsuitable for nesting. Even in Ireland many of our shorebirds, and especially waders, are declining as breeding species and if serious action is not taken soon we will be in danger of losing them. The shores of Western Europe are undergoing rapid change also with the intertidal landscape seeing warm-water species increasing, and existing species disappearing. Weather patterns are also changing quickly, affecting

Global warming will have a far-reaching effect on Ireland's shorebirds.

the ability of shorebirds to migrate successfully. With sea levels rising faster than before it is hard to see how shorebirds will cope with such a rapidly changing landscape, as feeding and roosting sites disappear. Like stepping stones, many places between breeding and wintering grounds are often relied on by shorebirds, vital for their safe passage. If any of these stepping stones is lost through global warming or other human activities the future of these astonishing creatures will be in doubt.

The places where our shorebirds live are coming under increasing pressure from many forms of human activity. Simple things like the increase in the number of people walking on the shore has resulted in increased pressure on shorebirds that need to feed and roost in these areas and do not have alternatives. Something that seems harmless, such as dogs running free on the shore, can add enormously to this pressure. Some people view the shore as a playground and unfortunately do not appreciate or value its natural beauty. The recent increase in the use of quad bikes on seashore habitat is not only disturbing our shorebirds but also destroying habitat.

Hunting also adds to the pressure. In the EU alone, where legislation is relatively strict, 5 goose species, 18 duck species, 11 wader species and 5 gull species can be legally shot at some time during a given year. Compared to most EU countries, Irish law affords reasonable protection for most shorebirds. Unfortunately, as you have read in this book, most of 'our' shorebirds migrate through many countries, some of which do not protect them as well as we do. For example, in Ireland the only waders on the hunting list are golden plover, snipe, jack snipe and curlew. In France for example, less than a day's shorebird flight from here for most of our waders, thirteen wader species can be legally shot. This, coupled with uncontrolled shooting in non-EU jurisdictions along their migrating pathways, adds to the natural pressures with which these birds have to contend from season to season.

It has been shown that some species seem to be able to withstand part of this pressure but the long-term view suggests that pressure on their wintering grounds from hunting and other causes will continue to grow and it remains to be seen if they can continue to absorb such pressure. If these birds are not afforded protection on their breeding and wintering grounds as well as along the total length of their migration flyways they will always be at risk.

In 21st century Ireland few people rely on the hunting of shorebirds for food or their survival. We would hope that the advent of digital photography and the accessibility to cheaper, high-powered lenses might persuade traditional hunters to swap their guns for cameras and capture the beauty of these birds on screen instead of killing or disturbing them. There is as much skill involved in capturing a good image of a shorebird with a camera as there is in killing one with a gun, and the bird remains alive after it has been 'shot' with the click of the camera shutter.

While the shore is a place for us to enjoy in many ways, we should be able to do so without endangering our incredible shorebirds that help make it a beautiful place to visit. Before anyone becomes concerned about the future of our shorebirds and where they live, they must first learn to appreciate and value them. We hope that books such as this one go some way towards achieving that goal. Once we are armed with the knowledge and insight, it is important that we have places where it is possible to watch shorebirds where they are safe and undisturbed. We need a network of wetland reserves around the island where people can go to watch and learn about these remarkable birds, away from traffic and disturbance. Estuary and coastal reserves are very popular in other countries and there is no doubt they would be here, too. They are not only safe havens for our shorebirds but can become important local amenities and contribute to our hard pressed economy through tourism.

It is not all doom and gloom. The current generation of schoolchildren in Ireland and abroad is being made far more aware of the consequences of our actions on our environment than those who currently run our country; there are many initiatives, such as An Taisce's Green Schools Programme, that are having a positive effect on our view of our environment, including the value of our natural heritage. The future of our shorebirds is in our hands. Let us hope we can secure their future and, in doing so, help to secure our own.

Facing page, top:
More and more people are using our shores for recreation. Striking the balance with the needs of our shorebirds will be an increasing problem.

Middle:
Can our wetlands survive in our world?

Bottom:
We need more coastal nature reserves like the excellent RSPB reserve in Belfast Harbour.

This black-tailed godwit was colour-ringed by Láki Sigurbjörnsson on his farm in northern Iceland in 2002 and has been seen in Ireland, France and England since then and, like the swallows in Ireland, has returned to Láki's farm each year since 2002 to breed.

Bibliography

A&C Black and Gibbon Multimedia, *RSPB Birds of Britain & Ireland Interactive PC and PDA* Edition Version 1.1, (London 2005).

Alerstam T., Christie D. A., Ulfstrand A., *Bird Migration,* (Cambridge 1993).

An Rionn Oideachais, *Ainmeacha Plandaí agus Ainmhithe,* (Dublin, 1978).

Arctic Shorebird Migration Workshop Bulletin 11 December 2006.

Anon. *Estuarine and Coastal Waters, (EPA 2004.).*

Boyd H., Petersen A., 'Spring Arrivals of Migrant Waders in Iceland in the 20th Century', *Ringing & Migration* (2006) 23, pp. 107–115.

Burenhult G., *The Archaeology of Carrowmore: Environmental Archaeology and Megalithic Tradition at Carrowmore, Co. Sligo,* (Stockholm, 1984).

Burton N. H. K., Rehfisch M., Clark N. A., Dodd S. G., 'Impacts of Sudden Winter Habitat Loss on the Body Condition and Survival of Redshank *Tringa totanus*', *Journal of Applied Ecology,* Vol. 43; No. 3, pp. 464–473(Oxford, 2006).

Campbell B., Lack E., *A Dictionary of Birds (*Calton 1985).

Clark J. A., 'Ringing Recoveries Confirm Higher Wader Mortality in Severe Winters', *Ringing & Migration* (2004) 22, pp. 43–50.

Crowe 0., *Ireland's Wetlands and their Waterbirds: Status and Distribution* (Wicklow, 2005).

De Courcy Ireland, J., *Ireland's Sea Fisheries: A History,* (1981).

Deal K. H., *Wildlife & Natural Resource Management* 2nd edition (New York, 2002).

Delany S., Scott D., Dodman T., Stroud D., *An Atlas of Wader Populations in Africa and Western Eurasia* (Wageningen, 2009).

Department of Animal Biology, Faculty of Sciences, Lisbon University, Lisbon., *The Use of Intertidal Areas by Foraging Waders: Constraints on the Exploitation of Food Resources* (Lisbon, 2009).

Dodd, S., *Weight Loss in Dunlin* Calidris alpina *over the High Tide Period.* Wader Study Group Bull. 91:28–29 2000.

Ehrlich P. R., Dobkin D. S., Wheye D., *Shorebird Communication* (Stanford, 1988).

Ehrlich P. R., Dobkin D. S., Wheye D., *Duck Displays* (Stanford 1988).

Estrella, S. M., *Behavioural and Feeding Mechanisms Flexibility in Migratory Shorebirds* (Spain, 2006).

Gibbons et al., *The New Atlas of Breeding Birds in Britain and Ireland 1988–1991 (*Carlton,1993).

Ginn H. B., Melville D. S., *Moult in Birds* l (Tring, 1983).

Greenberg R., Marra P. P., *Birds of Two Worlds: the Ecology and Evolution of Migration* (Baltimore, 2005).

Greenoak F., *All the Birds of the Air* (London, 1975).

Hagemeijer & Blair, *The EBCC Atlas of European Breeding Birds: Their Distribution and Abundance* (1997).

Harrison C., *A Field Guide to the Nests, Eggs and Nestlings* of British and European Birds (London, 1975).

Hayman P., Marchant J., Prater T., *Shorebirds – An Identification Guide to the Waders of the World* (Kent, 1986).

Hayward P. J., Nelson-Smith T., Shields C., *Sea Shore of Britain and Europe (Collins Pocket Guide* (London, 1996).

Hutchinson C. D., *Birds in Ireland* (Calton, 1989).

Hutchinson C.D., *Ireland's Wetlands and their Birds* (Dublin, 1979).

Irving B., *Technical Report: Fish Scales from Ferriter's Cove, County Kerry, Eire* (York, 1994).

Jong-Deock Lim, Zhou, Z. Martin L. D., Baek K.-S., Yang S.-Y., *The Oldest Known Tracks of Web-footed Birds from the Lower Cretaceous of South Korea*, Naturwissenschaften, Volume 87, No. 6 /June 2000, pp. 256–259 (Heidelberg, 2000).

Jonsson L., *Birds of Europe with North Africa and the Middle East* (London, 1992).

Lack P., *The Atlas of Wintering Birds in Britain and Ireland* (Calton, 1986).

Maclean I. M., Austin G. E., 'Waterbirds, Climate Change and Wildlife Conservation in Britain', *British Wildlife* April 2009, Vol. 20, No. 4, pp. 250–256.

Mieszkowska N., 'Sentinels of Climate Change – Species of the Rocky Intertidal Zone', *British Wildlife* April 2009, Vol. 20, No. 4, pp. 229–235.

Miller E. H., 'Antiquity of Shorebird Acoustic Displays' *Auk* April 2009, Vol. 126, No. 2, pp. 454–459.

Mitchell P. I., Newton S., Ratcliffe N., Dunn T.E. (eds.), *Seabird Populations of Britain and Ireland* (London, 2004).

Moriarty C., *A Guide to Irish Birds* (Cork, 1967).

Nienke Beintema N., *The Mysteries of Bird Migration* AEWA Secretariat.

Ó Caomhánaigh C., *Dictionary of Bird Names in Irish* (Dublin, 2002).

O'Sullivan A., Breen C., *Maritime Ireland: An Archaeology of Coastal Communities: Coastal Archaeology of an Island People* (Stroud, 2007).

Otte M. L. (Editor), *Wetlands of Ireland Distribution, Ecology, Uses and Economic Value* (Dublin, 2003).

Piersma T., & Lindström Å., 'Migrating Shorebirds as Integrative Sentinels of Global Environmental Change' *Ibis*, Vol. 146 Issue 1, pp. 61–69 (Published Online: 2004).

Rehfisch M., Austin G., Musgrove A., *Wintering Waders in Decline* (Bird Populations 7: pp. 162–165., 2003).

Ruttledge R. F., *A List of the Birds of Ireland* (Dublin, 1975).

Rynne C., *The Archaeology of Cork City and Harbour* (Cork, 1993).

Sample G., *Bird Songs and Calls of Britain and Northern Europe* (London, 1996).

Sheppard, R., *Ireland's Wetland Wealth – the Birdlife of the Estuaries, Lakes, Coasts, Rivers, Bogs and Turloughs of Ireland.*

The report of the Winter Wetlands Survey 1984/85 to 1986/87, (Dublin, 1993).

Scott, Derek A. and Rose, Paul M., *Atlas of Anatidae Populations in Africa and Western Eurasia* (Wageningen, 1996).

Snow, D. W. , Perrins, C. M., *The Birds of the Western Palearctic* Concise Edition, (Oxford 1998).

Staav, R. & Fransson, T., (2008) *EURING List of Longevity Records for European Birds* (http://www.euring.org/data_and_codes/longevity.htm).

Svensson L., Mullarney K., Zetterstrom D., *Collins Bird Guide* (London, 2000).

Tulp I., *The Arctic Pulse: Timing of Breeding in Long-Distance Migrant Shorebirds* (2007, Ph.D. Thesis, University of Groningen, The Netherlands).

van de Kam J., Ens B., Piersma T., Zwarts L., *Shorebirds: An Illustrated Behavioural Ecology,* (Utrecht, 2004).

Various Editors, *Irish Birds 1977–1993* (Dublin).

Various Editors, *British Wildlife 2000–2009* (Dorset)

Wernham C., Toms M., Marchant J., Clark J., Siriwardena G., and Baillie S., *The Migration Atlas Movements of the Birds of Britain and Ireland* (London, 2002).

Whitfield D. P., 'Raptor Predation on Wintering Waders in Southeast Scotland', *Ibis*, Vol. 127 Issue 4, pp. 544 – 558 (Published Online: 3 April 2008 Journal compilation © 2009 British Ornithologists' Union).

Wilson J. G., (ed.) *The Intertidal Ecosystem: The Value of Ireland's Shores*, pp. 38–44. Dublin: Royal Irish Academy. Coastal Wetland Birds and the EU Birds Directive (Oscar J. Merne).

Wilson J. R., *Sanderlings in Iceland.* Wader Study Group Bull.8 2: 44–45. (1997)

Zammuto R. M., *Life Histories of Birds: Clutch Size, Longevity, and Body Mass among North American Game Birds.* Can. J. Zool. 64: 2739-2749. (1986).

Bibliography for Iceland chapter

Arnalds, O., 2004. *Volcanic soils of Iceland.* Catena 56: 3–20.

Asbirk, S., Berg, L., Hardeng, G., Koskimies, P. & Petersen, A., 1997. 'Population sizes and trends of birds in the Nordic countries 1978–1994', *TemaNord* 614, Nordic Council of Ministers, Copenhagen.

Einarsson, M.A., 1984. *Climate of Iceland. World Survey of Climatology* (ed. H. Van Loon).

Elsevier, Amsterdam, New York. Pp. 673–697.

Gardarsson, A., 2006. *Recent Changes in Numbers of Cliff-breeding Seabirds in Iceland.* Bliki 27: 13–22. (In Icelandic with an English summary).

Gill, J. A., Norris, K., Potts, P. M., Gunnarsson, T. G., Atkinson, P. W. & Sutherland, W. J., 2001. 'The buffer effect and large-scale population regulation in migratory birds', *Nature* 412: 436–438.

Gudmundsson, G. A. & Gardarsson A.,1993. 'Numbers, geographic distribution and habitat utilization of waders (*Charadrii*) in spring on the shores of Iceland', *Ecography* 16: 82–93.

Gudmundsson, G. A., 2002. 'Estimates of populations of Icelandic waders.' Unpublished report for the International Wader Study Group. Icelandic Institute of Natural History, Reykjavík.

Gunnarsson, T. G., Gill, J. A., Þorlákur Sigurbjörnsson & Sutherland, W. J., 2004. 'Arrival synchrony in migratory birds', *Nature* 431: 646.

Gunnarsson, T. G., Gill, J. A., Ævar Petersen, Appleton, G. & Sutherland. W. J., 2005a. 'A double buffer effect in a migratory shorebird population', *Journal of Animal Ecology* 74: 965–971.

Gunnarsson, T. G., Gill, J. A., Newton, J., Potts, P. M. & Sutherland, W. J., 2005b. 'Seasonal matching of habitat quality and fitness in a migratory bird', *Proceedings of the Royal Society of London B* 272: 2319–2323.

Gunnarsson, T. G., Gill, J. A., Appleton, G. F., Hersir Gíslason, Arnthor Gardarsson, Watkinson A. R. & Sutherland, W. J., 2006. 'Large-scale habitat associations of birds in lowland Iceland: Implications for conservation', *Biological Conservation* 128: 265–275.

Gunnarsson, T. G., Gill, J. A., Atkinson, P. W., Gélinaud, G., Potts, P. M., Croger, R. E., Guðmundur A. Guðmundsson, Appleton, G. F. & Sutherland, W. J., 2006b. 'Population-scale drivers of individual arrival times in migratory birds', *Journal of Animal Ecology* 75: 1119–1127.

Gunnarsson, T. G., 2006c. 'Monitoring large-scale wader productivity during autumn passage in Iceland', *International Wader Study Group Bulletin* 109: 21–29.

Gunnarsson, T. G., 2009. 'Waders and wetlands in the light of land use', *Natturufraedingurinn* 79: 14–26. (In Icelandic with an English summary).

Hallsdottir, M., 1987. 'Pollen analytical studies of human influence on vegetation in relation to the Landnám tephra layer in Southwest Iceland', Lundqua thesis 18. Lund University, Lund. 45 pp.

Helgason, A., Sigurdardottir, S., Gulcher, J. R., Ward, R., & Stefansson, K., 2000a. 'mtDNA and the origin of the Icelanders: deciphering signals of recent population history', *American Journal of Human Genetics* 66: 999–1016.

Helgason, A., Sigurdardottir, S., Nicholson, J., Sykes, B., Hill, E. W., Bradley, D. G., Bosnes V., Gulcher, J. R., Ward, R. & Stefansson, K., 2000b. 'Estimating Scandinavian and Gaelic ancestry in the male settlers of Iceland', *American Journal of Human Genetics* 67: 697–717.

Icelandic Red List of Birds 2000. Icelandic Institute of Natural History. Reykjavík.

Ingolfsson, A., 1982. *Máfar kjóar og skúmar.* Fuglar, rit Landverndar 8. Reykjavík. [*Gulls and skuas*. Birds, book of the Land Protection Society, Reykjavík. In Icelandic].

Kristinsson, H., 1989. *Plöntuhandbókin.* *Íslensk Náttúra* 2. Örn og Örlygur. Reykjavík. P. 304. [*Handbook of Icelandic Plants*, Örn & Örlygur Press. In Icelandic].

Oskarsson, H., 1998. 'Framræsla votlendis á Vesturlandi', Í: *Íslensk votlendi, verndun og nýting* (ritstj. Jón S. Ólafsson). Háskólaútgáfan 283 bls. ['Wetland Drainage in West Iceland', in *Icelandic Wetlands* (ed. Olafsson, J. S.). University of Iceland Press, 1998. In Icelandic].

Thorhallsdottir, T. E., 2001. *Ásýnd landsins.* Ráðunautafundur 2001: 77–85 (in Icelandic).

Thorhallsdóttir, T. E., Jóhann Þórsson, Svafa Sigurðardóttir, Kristín Svavarsdóttir og Magnús H. Jóhannsson 1998. 'Röskun votlendis á Suðurlandi', Í: *Íslensk votlendi, verndun og nýting* (ritstj. Jón S. Ólafsson). Háskólaútgáfan 283 bls. ['Wetland Drainage in South Iceland', in *Icelandic Wetlands* (ed. Olafsson, J. S.). University of Iceland Press, 1998. In Icelandic].

Thorup, O. (ed.), 2006. 'Breeding waders in Europe 2000', *International Wader Studies* 14 (publication of the International Wader Study Group).

Useful Websites

www.antaisce.ie

http://alaska.usgs.gov/science/biology/shorebirds/index.html

www.artemis-face.eu/ (EU Bird Hunting Information Website)

www.birdsireland.com (Current Irish rare bird sightings and photos)

www.birdwatchgalway.org (BirdWatch Ireland Galway Branch)

www.birdwatchmayo.org (BirdWatch Ireland Mayo Branch)

www.birdwatchtipp.com (BirdWatch Ireland Tipperary Branch)

www.bto.org.uk (Bird conservation and research organisation)

http://www.bto.org/birdatlas/index.htm (Bird Atlas 2007 -11)

www.ring.ac (A website for reporting bird ring details)

www.birdlife.org

www.birdwatchireland.ie

www.birdweb.net (BirdWatch Ireland South Dublin Branch)

www.bwifingal.ie (BirdWatch Ireland Fingal Branch)

www.clarebirdwatching.com (BirdWatch Ireland Clare Branch)

www.cms.int (Bonn Convention on Migratory Species)

www.cr-birding.be/ (Information on colour-ringing schemes)

www.dublinbirding.ie (BirdWatch Ireland Tolka Branch)

www.dnfc.net (Dublin Naturalists' Field Club)

http://home.swipnet.se/~w-48087/faglar/materialmapp/dunlinmapp/
textmapp/caalpref2.html (the dunlin website)

www.enfo.ie (Information on the environment in Ireland)

www.epa.ie (Environmental Protection Agency)

http://www.euring.org/ (coordinating bird ringing throughout Europe)

www.fw.delaware.gov/Shorebirds/Pages/default.aspx

www.goose.org/main.html (International Goose Research Group)

www.greenshank.info

www.habitas.org.uk/bnfc/ (Belfast Naturalists' Field Club)

www.heritagecouncil.ie

http://home.scarlet.be/~pin02658/ (European colour-ring birding) www.ipcc.ie (Irish Peatland Conservation Council)

http://irishbrentgoose.org/ (Irish Brent Goose Research Group)

www.irishbirding.com/birds/web (Current Irish rare bird sightings and photos)

http://irbc.ie/ (Irish Rare Birds Committee)

www.iucn.org/ (International Union for Conservation of Nature)

www.iwt.ie (Irish Wildlife Trust)

www.jncc.gov.uk/page-3891 (Waterbirds Around the World)

http://migration.pwnet.org/pdf/Migration_Math_Madness.pdf

www.npws.ie (National Parks and Wildlife Service)

www.ramsar.org/ (The Ramsar Convention on Wetlands)

www.rspb.org.uk

www.scoiliosaefnaofa.com/Godwit.htm (Schools Godwit Project)

http://seaweed.ucg.ie/default.lasso

www.shorebirds.org.au/content/view/56/69/

www.sligobirding.com (BirdWatch Ireland Sligo Branch)

www.jncc.gov.uk/page-1548 (Results of Seabird 2000 Survey)

www.sovon.nl/ebcc/eoa (EBCC Atlas of European Breeding Birds)

www.uea.ac.uk/~b026515/ (Project Jadrakan – Black-tailed Godwits)

www.unep-aewa.org/ (African-Eurasian Migratory Waterbird Agreement) (AEWA)

www.waders.org

www.waderstudygroup.org (International Wader Study Group)

www.waterfordbirds.com

www.westcorkbirdwatch.zoomshare.com (BirdWatch Ireland West Cork Branch)

www.wetlands.org

www.wexfordnaturalists.com

www.wildlifetrusts.org

www.wwt.org.uk (Wildfowl and Wetland Trust)

A winter sunrise over an estuary at Belvelly, Cork Harbour.